PAGE ONE DIGEST
Volume II

An anthology of creative writing

From Newfoundland's West Coast

Published by

Cabbitt Productions

2018

Deer Lake, NL

Copyright 2018 Page One

Cabbitt Productions
59 North Main St
Suite 2
Deer Lake, NL
A8A 1N1

Editing: Chief Editors: D. Jean Young and Nellie P. Strowbridge
Assistant Editor: Marilyn Young
Assistant Proofreaders: Cynthia Babb Fry, Jean Legge Hiscock, Angela Parsons
Cover Design: Terry Gordon
Book Design: Angela Parsons
Pictures: D. Jean Young, Victoria Kawaja, P.J.Fernandez, Delaney Pelley, Samantha A. Parsons, Candice Curlew
Cabbitt Logo: Victoria Kawaja

The opinions of any individual author are not necessarily those of the Page One group or the publisher.

INTRODUCTION

Once upon a time in September, 1987, local writers met a visiting author in Corner Brook, Newfoundland and decided to set up a writers' group to support and encourage each other in their creative endeavours. After some debate, the writers decided to call this new unit, Page One. Three of the original members still play an important part in this group: Jean Legge Hiscock, D. Jean Young and Marilyn Young. Many people have come and gone over the years and many of our events and publications include writers and performers who have never or rarely attended a meeting. We have had student employees each summer since 1987. We have employed people under JCP and New Horizons grants. The group is ad hoc in many ways and has no formalized structure or board. And yet, we have continued to exist for more than 30 years. That creates the question: ***Who are the members of Page One?*** In my opinion, anyone who wants to be considered a member is welcome. We are inclusive rather than exclusive. The more an individual participates, the more benefits that person receives.

Our pot luck suppers are informal and fun and, perhaps, we do not pay enough attention to the craft of writing. However, the storytelling is always present and often ends up in a poem or a prose piece. Open mics with supper included in the price surprise people with local talent from authors and musicians. Our annual **Summer Voices** events include artists and authors in collaborative experience. One **Sounds of Youth** group made a movie and another hosted a concert. Page One has hosted an evening for ghost stories and a Murder Mystery Dinner Theatre. Page One encourages intergenerational projects. For example, this book includes authors who are six and authors who are in their nineties and those of all ages in between. Some projects focus on children, or teenagers or seniors. Page One is for anyone who wants to create and wants to share. New ideas and participants are welcome.

Under Cabbitt Productions, we have published these collections of works by many authors: ***Page One Digest, Volume 1; A Christmas Journey;***

Love, Lust, Laughter; Gap/Spanners; Thursday 13th; Handbook to Making Your Golden Years Golden. This book will be our newest production.

Under Byrn-Out Productions, we have published: individual collections by Fred Stewart (*This, That and the Other Thing*) and Rudy Campbell (*Alchemist*) and an autobiographical book by Terry Manuel (*Walking into Paradise.*)

This book is a compilation from a wide variety of people. Some have never had their work published before. Nellie P. Strowbridge is a well known author of books, an advice column, a research column and winner of many awards. Others fall in between in skill and publication history. We have included work from writers who are no longer with us in this world. Some were active members and some we have never met in person but have had their work passed on to us by family. Our goal is preserve the voices of our creators in a permanent collection to be enjoyed and not lost in dusty closets, or, heaven forbid, the garbage heap. Cry, laugh, think, enjoy as you flip through the pages. You never know what you will find. *You will see dates at the end of poems or prose pieces. These are the dates of the births and deaths of our contributors*.

Following our tradition of adding Newfoundland sayings, traditions and humour, you will see short entries at the bottom of pages scattered throughout the book. You may have heard the jokes before; smile anyway.

Gathering Words includes poetry and prose about Page One, the writing process, and a reading at Word on the Street.

I Remember takes the reader down through the roads of memory, of times that used to be, and the longing we feel when we remember what used to be.

Cold Sensations explores the darker side of life from a variety of viewpoints.

Ouch includes writing from a six-year-old and excerpts from a session at an elementary school many years ago. You will be sure to smile at their imagined dream houses.

Let Me Sing for You Anyhow talks about relationships between families, couples, friends, and pets and, well, you will have to read the last poem to see what means the most to that writer.

'Twix the Sea and the Sky is a collection of poems and prose about connections to nature and land and how it shapes our world views.

Imagine There's No Limit is a Cabbitt Stew, an assortment of pieces without a specific uniting theme, similar to the mixture that is Page One.

Read, enjoy, and consider joining our group or putting your pen to paper and writing your own poem, story, essay or choose to take a photo or draw or paint. We may be happy to share it in a future publication or at one of our events. And, if you prefer, come along to our events and listen and look. We need audiences, too!

The origin of the CABBITT: In 1997, Page One received a Cabot 500 grant and we decided we wanted our own logo. At a meeting, we considered a number of options and Daphne Russell told a side story of a cat who mated with a rabbit and produced offspring – a cabbitt. As a group that embraces strange and wild ideas and yet is really quite tame and domestic, a Cabbitt seemed to be a perfect choice. We had no images of such a creature. Victoria Young rose to the challenge and created our mascot and our trademark: The white Cabbitt. Part cat, part rabbit, you never know what to expect from this mystical creation.

Acknowledgements

Thank you to the following:

Government Assistance: New Horizons for Seniors, JCP, SWASP, Canada Student Summer
Media coverage: Western Star, K-Rock, VOCM, OZ FM, CBC and CFCB, Envision, ca.

General Support: DJY Financial and Spillway Connections for providing office space, equipment, guidance and supervision.

DEDICATION

To all who

have contributed to Page One:

authors, artists, musicians and our

audience: readers, viewers and listeners

Table of Contents

GATHERING WORDS..**1**

What Poets Do: Vaughn Harbin **2**

Page One: Daphne Russell.............................. **3**

My Story: Florence Antle **4**

The Book: Marilyn Young................................ **5**

How to Write A Poem: Fred Stewart **6**

Inspired by her Poem Alzheimer's Voice: Dana Cole **7**

The Reading on Pier 21: Robert Parsons.............. **9**

I REMEMBER.... .... **11**

The Lure of Newfoundland: Fred Stewart **12**

Remembering Port Aux Basques: Marjorie Patey **14**

Life's Revolving Doors: Minnie J. Vallis................ **15**

Memory Road: Anne Bowring **18**

Excerpt from "When The Newfie Bullet Went Bang": Ronald T. Smith..**20**

Berry-Picking: Ruth Young............................. **21**

The Christmas Pudding: Shirley Dyke................. **22**

Campbellton Man: Matthew Spence **23**

The Fisher's Grace: George T. Tucker **24**

When the Fishin' Was Good: George T. Tucker **26**

In Case I Need to Save the World: Cynthia Babb Fry **28**

An Old Friend: G.M. Legge **29**

Uncle Joe: Fred Stewart............................... **30**

Diana: Florence Antle................................. **32**

Stuart McLean: Jackie Sheppard Alcock.............. **33**

The Piano: Daisy Bennett-Lush **35**

Watch the Ashes Fall: Jean Legge Hiscock............ **38**

COLD SENSATIONS 39

Swimming Lesson: Jean Legge Hiscock 40
My Journey: Trina King 41
Hunger: Nico LaBlanc 44
Reading Coffee Grounds: Nellie P. Strowbridge........ 45
He Was My Nightmare: Jennifer Sutton 46
My Soul, My House: Deborah Hedd 48
Cold: Florence Antle.................................... 51
A Silent Love: Terry Manuel............................ 50
The Uncanny: Norma Jean House...................... 51
"Exhausted": Jamie Stuckless 59
Not A Bedtime Story: Nellie P. Strowbridge 60
Feed My Addiction: Francis King 64
Dear Sis: Julie LeClair.................................. 65
Woman on The Street: Jean Legge Hiscock 77
The Big "C": Deborah Hedd.......................... 78

OUCH! 81

My Ouch Story: Aaron Kawaja 82
My Dream House: Elementary Students (1997-1998) 84

LET ME SING TO YOU ANYHOW 87

The Wait: Nellie P. Strowbridge 88
Surrogate Creator: Nellie P. Strowbridge.............. 89
Small One: Jamie Stuckless............................ 90
Kristen: Stacey Hiscock-Pittman 91
Momma: Kayla Critch................................... 92
My Dad Was a Miner: Cynthia Babb Fry 93
I Remember Her Still: Ray Bennett 95
A Salted Soul?: Minnie J. Vallis 96
Spring Pleasures: Nico LaBlanc........................ 97
A New Beginning: Natasha Strickland.................. 98

Not Kissing Cousins: Deborah Hedd **100**

A Pastel Hymn: Matthew Spence **102**

Between You and Me: Terry Manuel **103**

Album of Love: Arthur Ball **104**

Love Is Love: Deanna Mcdeiros **105**

Desire: Terry Manuel **107**

Love Your Mom & Dad: Daphne Russell **108**

My Mother: Florence Antle **109**

A Vision of an Independent Writer: Anne Bowring **110**

Twice Loved: Karen Bennett **114**

A Trapper's Wife: George T. Tucker **116**

The Gun and the Door: Nellie P. Strowbridge **117**

Current Affair: Fred Stewart **121**

The Life of a Flower: Jackie Sheppard Alcock **122**

Unbalanced: Daisy Bennett-Lush **123**

Chaos: Roxanne Abbott **124**

What Is That Racket?: Ray Bennett **125**

Dump Kitty: Kayla Critch **127**

Wistful: Cynthia Babb Fry **128**

Mirrors and Boxes: Nellie P. Strowbridge **129**

Points of Light: Karen Bennett **137**

Father and Son: Daphne Russell **138**

The Tailrace Clowns: Daphne Russell **140**

A Poem at The Manor: Myrtle Hutchings **141**

The Light of My Life: Fred Stewart **144**

'TWIX THE SEA & THE SKY **145**

Home: Natasha Strickland **146**

The Cabin: Hilda King **147**

Amazing Bird: Annie Gillard **148**

Swallow: Nico LaBlanc **150**

Chickadee: Karen Bennett **151**

Seasons: Nico LaBlanc **152**

Drawn: Vaughn Harbin **154**

Across the Mesh: Deborah Hedd **155**

Blindness: Nico LaBlanc **166**

Hearts That Give Heed to The Sea: Vaughn Harbin **168**

"Leave Me These!": Vaughn Harbin **168**

Our Home: Dana Cole **169**

The Vision: As Told To Greg Alexander **171**

The Line 'Twix The Sea and The Sky: Jean Legge Hiscock **173**

Ocean: Desmond Russell **174**

The Gulch: Mike Madigan **175**

Baby Tree: Terri Hayden(Moores) **176**

Timber Moose: Jean Legge Hiscock **177**

The Lovely Spud: G. M.Legge **178**

To A Chick: Jean Legge Hiscock **179**

The Great White Hunter: David Elliott **180**

Soup: Jean Legge Hiscock **185**

Freedom: Hilda King **186**

IMAGINE THERE'S NO LIMIT **187**

A Toast to Trucks: Karen Bennett **188**

Choices: Dana Cole **189**

My Trip: Sarah Lynn Bussey **191**

Fear Aboard the Airplane: Edith Johnson **194**

Woman of Colour: Nellie P. Strowbridge **199**

Accidental Newfie: Selwyn Skiggs **200**

Dieter's Paradox: David Elliott **202**

Connivers: Norma Jean House **203**

Crime Pays: Jean Legge Hiscock **204**

Early Morning Shower: Daisy Bennett-Lush **205**

The Half Brother: Fred Stewart **209**

The Glass of Pepsi: Stacey Hiscock-Pittman **210**

Ed Dethroned!: Marilyn Young **211**

When the Deal Is Down: Minnie J. Vallis **212**

Through the Eyes of an Angel: Terri-Lynn Shugarue **218**

God Speaks: Natasha Strickland **223**

Faith: G. M. Legge **223**

Fellowship: Dana Cole **224**

Imagine: Brittney Stuckless **225**

The Special Light: Julie Crocker **226**

Cemetery Road: John Tuach **227**

Guest of Honour: Jean Legge Hiscock **228**

Gathering Words

What Poets Do

I write the truth.
I dare do so
For I am a poet
And that is what poets do.

There is freedom in the pen
Power and
Responsibility.

With my pen I am free
To write what is true.

I have the power,
And I must!
For I am a poet
And that is what poets do.

~ *Vaughn Harbin*

Page One

Page One is a local group in Western Newfoundland
Who love to get together every now and then
To talk about our writing and maybe read aloud,
We have more to talk about when there's a larger crowd.

Some of us write short stories, a poem or a song.
We invite more people to be interested and to come along.
To share each other's words each night,
To hear what each will say.
There's room for others; why not come our way?

It really can be lots of fun for the young and for the old.
We can't promise any writers they will reach their goals.
We'll do our best and welcome you, if you will come in.
And join our little writers' group in Western Newfoundland.

We have faith in each other; this is how we hope to stay.
We will do the best we can in every way.
So dear writers, join us and see what we can be.
We are Page One; we could be Page Two or Three.

~ *Daphne Russell*

My Story

My mother asked me to write about my life
Of all the hardships, the struggles and strife.
She said, "If you're able to tell about your pain,
Maybe then you'll be ready to live again."

"I know it will be hard to relive the past.
You can do it, I know you can, lass."
I thought about this and wondered if I would -
Another big question, if I really should?

The years have slipped by
And I wonder, should I let sleeping dogs lie?
If telling my story will help me some way,
Maybe I will do it; maybe I'll have my say.

~ Florence Antle

If your gut instinct tells you to make a certain choice in simple matters, such as what trump to bid on in a game of cards or in making a life-changing decision, Newfoundlanders will advise you to go with the strategy that comes to you first, or, to put it simply, "Follow your first mind."

The Book

As writers, all of us imagine the time when
We write the "magic book" that will give us
Fame and Fortune.

Few of us remember - through the minutes,
The hours, days and months of struggle that it is
Oftentimes, not ourselves only who will make us
Famous - but literary agents, publishers, and
Of course, what we require most - readers.

While being a published author may be our true aim,
Whoa, our heartfelt desire!
May we never forget the joy of those snatches of time
Spent writing much shorter versions of shared experiences.

What we also oftentimes forget, as we strive
To get phrases, sentences, pages and chapters
Written that what we do as writing exercises can
Become, if compiled, into one literary piece -
That Elusive Book.

~ *Marilyn Young*

How to Write A Poem

I'd like to start this little rhyme
By saying, "Once upon a time."
This story isn't true, you see,
I really think it ought to be.
There was a man who tried to write
A poem; he tried with all his might.
He tried by day and he tried by night.
He couldn't get it rhyming right.
He searched the dictionary through
To find a work that rhymed with blue.
He asked his wife and children too
If they could rhyme a word with blue.
They shook their heads and said, "If you
Can't find a word to rhyme with blue
Don't ask us. That's hard to do,
To find a work to rhyme with blue."
And so he went away and wept,
And then he closed his eyes and slept.
He had a dream, a vision true –
He dreamed he rhymed a word with blue.
He quickly woke all in a sweat
To write it down lest he forget.
He snapped the lacing in his shoe
And forgot the word that rhymed with blue.
And so he studied quite some time
The art of making poems rhyme.
At last one morning he could say,
"I'm going to write a poem today."
He started out his little rhyme
By saying, "Once upon a time."

~ *Fred Stewart*
1934 – 2007)

A Tribute to Nellie P. Strowbridge

Sometimes when people speak, we hear what they don't say louder than what they do say. Nellie P. Strowbridge is an inspiration to many.

Inspired by her Poem
Alzheimer's Voice
Shadows of the Heart, 1998

It's strange how quickly
we can complete a circle:
some of us losing minds
it took us almost a century to fill
with memories of scents and scenes,
as we went from the babbling voice of a baby
to where our tongues strung words
together like pearls.
Now it is difficult to gather words
in beautiful expression and
harder to decipher
other people's strings of words.
They lie broken in a pool of memories
inside a dark room.
We speak anyway, words on top of words,
hoping we will find new life in them,
ears for them,
and recognition in someone's eyes.

Until I read your poem I did not realize I would hear a voice able to speak about the way things are. I realized life changes; it cannot stay the same; sister to brother, brother to sister; you have given a voice to feelings hard to express, letting others see that we all have needs; you understand that to handle burdens, sharing is essential.

To quote a friend: "Are we a result of chaos or are we under the control of a higher power as we share this rock dangling in space?" I admit it takes faith to consider the latter the truth. I believe we are our brothers' and sisters' keepers. Sometimes, listening can be the best thing we can do. Take it from someone who's been there. We've all been touched by trouble to some degree.

Thank you, Nellie and others who share. Your voice activated a response in me I didn't know I had. I write you to say: Right on, Nellie, write on, launch your books. I want to read what you have to write. I have been given a new appreciation for the written words, across the pages. You've lightened my load by strengthening its carrier. I have lost battles and companions, yet I am thankful for your words of encouragement.

I will keep on, the heartache and pain kicked out of the caboose of this train, as I proceed to the heavenly place where I will see Him and understand everything.

Nellie, you're not a writer because you write; you write because you are a writer.

Your book *Shadows of the Heart,* sharing some of your life with us, made me see. It reminded me that faith is an action word.

Thank you for sharing your wealth of knowledge and for understanding the human spirit. Thank you, Nellie.

~ *Dana Cole*

The Reading on Pier 21

A little over ten years ago I was selected to go to Halifax to read at the annual Fall gathering of Word on the Street, attended each year by several thousand people. In the early years, the event was held on Spring Garden Road. Now it is housed and held on the waterfront at Pier 21.

Years ago, from about 1928 to the 1970s, immigrants by the hundreds poured through Pier 21 as they entered Canada for the first time. It was similar to Ellis Island of New York in the early 1900s.

I attended Word on the Street with my pre-teen son and read from an unpublished short story about a Nova Scotian vessel called *Milton*.

Tents, booths, clowns, snack tables, book sellers, buyers, costumes, music, magic, readings, all made the building buzz with activity. People milled around, mixing with authors, would-be authors and publishers. They sat in tents listening to authors read from their work: fiction, non-fiction, poetry, children's books, cookbooks, you name it.

My son looked at the schedule and noted that I was scheduled for the non-fiction booth at 1:20 PM.

"See it's between the children's literature venue and the coffee shop," he said pointing. "I want to get to your reading. I'll be over to listen. Then I'll let you know how you did, honestly, if you picked the right passages and if you looked up and if you smiled and—"

"Right, Son," I said, waving him away.

I had lots of time, so I sat back in the Lifestyles tent, ready to listen to Bruce Nunn. He's the CBC guy in Halifax who digs up and reports on local history with a twist. Bruce read a good story about the only male Nova Scotian soldier in World War II who wore a skirt. The guy was part of the army's entertainment group. A general fell for the man in lady's disguise. Nunn was about to get to the good part on how the soldier wiggled out of that one when someone tapped me on the shoulder.

"Aren't you supposed to be over there, reading?"

It was Fred, a cousin from my hometown, Grand Bank. He had come up from Dartmouth to Halifax to Word on the Street in Pier 21 to socialize and listen to me.

"Get to the non-fiction booth," he said. "It's a little after 1:20, and I'm waiting to hear you read."

I grabbed my book, rushed up to the stage and microphone and began to read. Perhaps I looked up, smiled, told the right story – one about the tragedy of the ship *Milton*.

When the reading was over, I chatted with Fred about family and things back home. I thanked him for the tap on the shoulder and the reminder. I had been so engrossed with Nunn's reading, I almost missed my own reading.

Fred and I parted, each to wander around the various venues.

Several minutes later I bumped into my son and asked, "Well, how did I do on my reading?"

"Your reading, Dad?"

"Yes, you know. Non-fiction booth, 1:20 this afternoon."

"Oh, Dad, sorry. I was over at another venue and I heard this person reading. It was such an interesting story; I became totally engrossed."

~ Robert Parsons

I Remember....

The Lure of Newfoundland

What is it about that misshapen Rock
That entices its children to roam,
Then creates within them an obsessive urge
To leave where they are and go home?

The yearning is there every day of the year,
Especially strong in Spring,
When thoughts turn back to those long-ago joys
That Summertime there used to bring.

For a Newfie's home will always be there,
On the island that gave him his life,
The place that he left, his fortune to seek,
Where he lived well, free from strife.

Those joyful, carefree days of his youth
He never again is to know
As long as he strays from his island home
Where the warm South Westerlies blow.

For he finds the world a big fearful place,
Not like his home on the Rock
And the stress of simply staying alive
Sends him into a quick state of shock.

Then he realizes what he left behind
As the longing gets greater each day
To get away from his surrogate home
To his real home by the bay.

And he knows if he doesn't, he's doomed to die
Alone in a foreign place
Where no one knows where he belongs
And no one remembers his face.
'Tis a sad, sad thing when this happens to him
And that is the reason why
I'm going back home to live on my Rock
And be buried right there when I die.

~ *Fred Stewart*
(1934 - 2007)

An easy way to bravely jump into cold water for a swim is to go in quickly until you in are up to your waist and shout, "Hens, turkeys, chickens, DUCK!" and sink into the chilly waters up to your chin. When the numbness wears off, the water will feel much warmer.

Remembering Port Aux Basques

I was sixteen years old
When I wanted to roam
I picked Port aux Basques
And called it my home

I worked in the fish plant
made many new friends
The memories I'll cherish
Until my life ends

Every night we went to Harry Tom's
To play the harmonica and listen to songs

Port aux Basques is a nice place
Yes, that is true
The people are friendly
Always there for you

You drive downtown
a very nice view to see
Watch the Marine Atlantic boats
Come in from the sea

When my life is over
And they lay me to rest
I want to stay in Port aux Basques
The place I love best

My poem now has ended
I have nothing more to say
I am a proud Newfoundlander
From Lally Cove, Fortune Bay

~ Marjorie Patey

Life's Revolving Doors

It has been written, "As the twig is bent, the tree's inclined." I question if this applies to the human family. Where does personality come into the picture?

As we ripen with age and look back at our yesteryears, I wonder if the old saying "the more things change, the more they stay the same" is more applicable to families and life itself. You, the reader, can be the judge.

I vividly remember my first day of school. My mother used a ribbon to tie up my massive ringlets that hung over my shoulders My school bag, made from flour bags, contained my slate pencil, a small bottle of water and a piece of cloth to keep the slate clean. I proudly swung the bag over my shoulder and walked off to school.

I was very excited to enter the two-room, two-storey wooden structure with painted floors. I didn't mind that there was no running water. We had a two-room outhouse.

Clang, clang, clang went the school bell. What a delightful sound!

I was eager and totally amazed that, in this huge building, I would learn about our big world. The boats, winds, tides and stars were a mysterious combination. I learned that some cities were so large that the island I grew up on, population around three hundred, could fit neatly into a few city blocks and be barely noticeable. I learned that the grass in Scotland were many shades of green and much more beautiful than the few patches that grew on our rocky island.

I had a great love of people and was told about the many languages in this world. I vowed to learn every language and become a travelling nurse so I could help those who were sick and often sad through their illnesses.

School had one regulation. If you had an older brother or sister in the same classroom you sat beside him or her for the first few days. My sister, who was almost five years older than me, was not extremely fond of me. She had difficulty reading and although I was just starting school I could read many words and sentences; she was gifted in the art of drawing pictures. Sitting beside my sister, I was given a whispered order: "Keep your bloody little paws off my books."

I could not draw pictures, but I did not mind. I had broken pieces of dishes in my rock playhouse and I often served tea and mud cookies to the king and queen of England who never made any requests for me to draw a picture.

"Good morning Primers," the teacher said. "Here's your first job. I want you to do your very best work; I'll correct it shortly."

With a stick of chalk, and a few quick strokes on the blackboard, the teacher drew a mother duck with three baby ducks behind her; underneath the four ducks were wavy lines that resembled water. I tried and I cried.

Then my sister hit me with her elbow and whispered, "I'll draw it for you. Don't tell the teacher."

Well, I took the vow of silence, crossed my heart and hoped to die if I told the teacher my sister did my drawing.

For her, like the teacher, a few quick strokes on the slate and the job was completed. It seemed to be an eternity before the teacher got back to the Primers class (kindergarten did not exist in my school days. The teacher was finally beside my desk admiring the work of art. I waited for her question: Did you draw this yourself? I was ready to say yes. The question did not come.

Instead, the teacher said, "Your sister is really good at drawing pictures isn't she?"

I quickly replied, "Oh, yes, I wish I could draw as well as that."

I was not prepared for that sort of trick, or trap. My sister told me she would have to stay behind during recess period and miss one ball game. She whispered that she owed me a lickin'.

She cried after school telling our parents what had happened when she had tried to help me.

Dad suggested: "From here on my dear, don't ask your sister to lie about things. It's best you not do it for her; let her stand on her own feet and learn to accept the fact that all of us have strong points. All of us also have some weaker points in life too."

Life is different now. I will readily admit to my offspring that if I, at their age, would have had to complete a certain project I would have needed some assistance. My offspring so often share news of their great accomplishments with me. If they received help, they will mention who it was that assisted them.

I am inclined to believe that looking through the eyes of a child and now through the eyes of a grandmother that life is like revolving doors and "the more things change, the more they stay the same."

As for my dream of becoming a travelling nurse, the most I learned in the medical field was basic First Aid and CPR. As for learning every language that has been spoken I learned to speak but one, with great fluency - the truth. Where is the massive head of ringlets I once had? It's your turn to decide what the answer would be now.

Namaste.

~ Minnie J. Vallis
(1933 - 2013)

Mothers refused to let daughters wear red ribbons. According to a local story, an infant, wearing a red dress, was set out on her bridge (veranda) to get some sunshine. When her mother came out to check on her child, she had disappeared. Quietly, quickly, fairies. fascinated by the colour red, had stolen her away.

Memory Road

I remember walking the roads in Deer Lake when I was a young girl. Everything sure has changed.

It was a pleasant time. The limbs of high trees waved and pretty flowers lined the streets. Trains, across the road from Main Street, brought people in to see a doctor at the small hospital where the 50+ Club now has its building. Main Street was a lively place back then. Before the movie started, children who had any talent got in free and they step-danced and sang on the stage in front of the heavy velvet curtains hiding the screen below the fancy plaster ceilings.

Next door, Danny Joseph opened the Ambassador Club. To get in, you had to have a membership. Men worked in the woods camps and when they came home on weekends, they acted rowdy and threw a few punches. When Ranger Hogan came to town, he set down the law and cut down on the worst of the brawls.

The Mitchells sold furniture. Frances Joseph set up a clothing shop. We had restaurants and an ice cream parlour where we sat and talked over ice cream and sodas. Mr. Dunne opened a drug store and the Bank of Montreal opened a branch. Other stores were on or near Main Street, too: the Schwartzes, Wellons, Goodyears, and others. You could buy anything in the shopping area of town.

In the summer time, we ran to the swimming pool where the stadium parking lot is now. We danced in the wooden dance hall in the evenings, sat at the benches under the trees and went to church garden parties in St. Judes and Nicholsville. There were snacks sold at the garden parties, crafts and sometimes there was a Jumbo Sale (what they call a flea market now). On Labour Day, Deer Lake had a big time. They closed off Main Street from Morley Coish's, at the corner of Goodyear's Hill to Pennell's Lane and we enjoyed the street dances.

I remember people riding on the train to go berry-picking on the Gaff Topsails. We listened to the music on the way and had a grand time. The trip took a whole day. We also went to Corner Brook on the train to do our Christmas shopping.

Wintertime, we enjoyed ourselves on the old rink on Gatehouse Road. I'd put on my skates and skate all the way up

Middle Road, feeling so free! When hockey games were held at the rink, an old wood stove at the entrance helped us warm up.

We had no cell phones and no television. Telegrams delivered news, good and bad. Before Mom's brother came to visit from Grand Falls, he'd send a telegram. It was delivered by hand to our door. Bad news came that way, too. When a relative or good friend died, we heard the news first in a telegram.

We had no microwave oven. When we came home after school, Mom was in the kitchen; we always looked forward to a good meal.

People in those days were close. They depended on each other. These are some of the pictures I remember in my album of Memory Road.

~ *Anne Bowring*

If you lose an object, write your name on your forehead backwards and ask St. Anthony to help you. Recite this rhyme: "Good St. Anthony look around. Something's lost and must be found."

Excerpt from "When The Newfie Bullet Went Bang"

(First printed in Page One Digest, Volume 2, 1997)

The return trip [from Corner Brook to Deer Lake] is better [than the journey down]. Can it be because darkness has enveloped the entire scenario? A beautiful harvest moon dances through the clouds.

The shaft of a guitar protrudes through the opening of the adjacent compartment, and the sounds of "The Wild Rover" and "Blowing in the Wind" are muted as the train picks up speed. Near Pasadena, the accordion comes on stream with "The Squid Jiggin' Ground."

The train lurches and a fire extinguisher pops out of its strapping. The train hand shrugs and kicks it under a seat.

~ Ronald T. Smith

Berry-Picking

I remember when
      we could pick raspberries
      right out by our door.

One year, the children
      picked enough
      for me to make
      one hundred bottles of jam.

Not all the one time, now –
      just a dipperful at a time.

And one girl could pick berries
      when no one else
      could find any.

She would go out
      and pick a cupful for breakfast
      and put a bit of sugar
      over them.

It was the only breakfast
      she ever wanted.

We picked raspberries
      right out by our door,
      two gallons to make one.

~ Ruth Young
(1920 - 2003)

The Christmas Pudding

The aroma was filling the house as I stepped inside. I wondered what kind of pudding it was this year. Mom was always excited over her puddings. She had so many choices: Partridgeberry, Plum, Figgy Duff. Mom had everything all measured out and put to one side.

All of a sudden, I saw a bowl of partridgeberries, my favourite berry. I thought, Mom won't miss those berries. She had everything all ready for her pudding. I took the bowl and went to my room.

Soon the time came for the longed-for Christmas pudding. Mom was so excited, as she brought it out.

"We are having partridgeberry pudding," she said, carefully slicing the pudding. She stopped and stared. "Oh my God," she said, "I can't see any partridgeberries. They were all measured out with the other ingredients, but they're not here."

I felt so guilty, I crawled under the table and cried.

Poor Mom! She was called "Partridgeberry Free Pudding" after that.

~ Shirley Dyke

Two knives crossed on the table signals a fight will soon erupt.
A knife and a fork crossed on a plate, during a meal, indicates that the person has finished eating.

Campbellton Man

In early spring when I was young
I left my home for the middle of the woods.
We built log cabins with our naked hands,
A town grew up as I became a man.

We came from all around the coast.
We left our families and small wooden boats.
We said we'd be back with savings we'd earn,
But we were never able to return.

I said a Campbellton man I'd always be –
Can't take the salt water out of me.
I forgot how to fish as I learned how to log,
I forgot my church as I prayed to God.

The winter camps were very cold,
The savage winds and the deep dark snow.
All I had for a pillow was a chunk of birch
And my hands grew thick with the heavy work.

Now this island's wood has all been cleared,
My grandson will leave in the spring of the year.
He'll tell his grandchildren stories to help them understand
About growing up in Newfoundland

~ Matthew Spence

The Fisher's Grace

I remember when he took my hand
And walked down to the sea.
I remember how he looked that day
So quietly he looked at me.

There was a twinkle in his eyes
Lines etched in his face.
His gnarled hands a story told
As he sang the Fisher's Grace.

CH:
Don't take the sea away from me
Don't bar the old stage door.
Turn the fish on the flake
While I go out once more.

I remember when he let me go
Out on the briny sea.
I told him then and feel it now
There's no other place I'd rather be.

He let me steer old Mary Ann
And to the whales give chase.
He taught me how to mend the nets
And words of the Fisher's Grace.

CH:
Don't take the sea away from me
Don't bar the old stage door
Turn the fish on the flake
While I go out once more.

He taught me to respect the sea
How to turn into the wind
To listen to the seagulls' cry
To know when fishing begins.

As things started to settle down
A calm would cross his face.
He'd turn and smile at me
And sing the Fisher's Grace.

CH:
Don't take the sea away from me
Don't bar the old stage door
Turn the fish on the flake
While I go out once more.

The salt sea ran in his blood
And everyone could see
The tall tales he would tell
Were about Grandpa and me.

Now I have been out many times
His footsteps I would trace
And in the misty ocean calm
I could hear the Fisher's Grace.

CH: x2 repeat last 2 lines

~ George T. Tucker

When the Fishin' Was Good

I remember the days my Pa came in
His face lit with a mighty grin
Then from his lips a mighty hooray
And all in one breath he would say,
"There's lots of fish out there today."

I remember the stories he could tell
Of all the fish he brought home to sell
Quintals of fish, I recall,
Plenty for everyone there'll be this fall,
Down the gang plank he would walk
To the fish shed so full of talk,
And as he entered through the back door,
His wooden wheel barrow would creak the floor.
Everyone there understood
These were times when the fishin' was good.

Today my child asked of me,
"When did Grandpa die at sea?"
I gave him an answer as best I could,
"At a time when fishin' was good."

The seagulls are silent,
An empty wharf, on the water a boat or two.
So too, the shed from where the laughter did peel
And the old wooden barrow doesn't have even a wheel.
Try and try as much as we could,
There's no going back to a time
When the fishin' was good.

You see, there aren't enough fish to go around
Out there on the old fishing ground.
Our only hope, 'cause of the powers that be,
Is to pray for another food fishery
Times you could fish and get what you could
Was at a time when the fishin' was good.

~ *George T. Tucker*

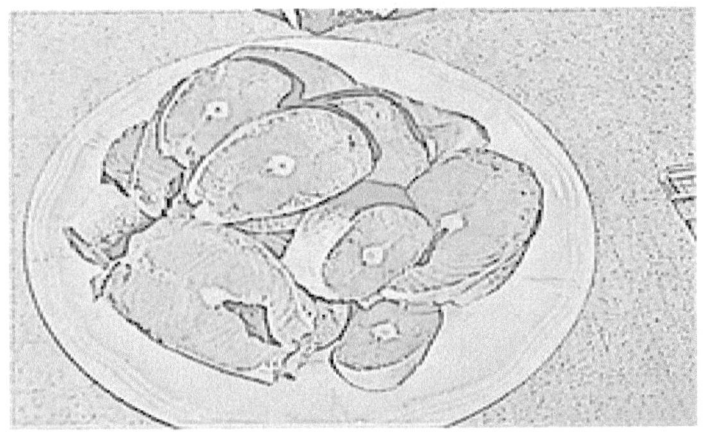

When the Fishing Was Good

In Case I Need to Save the World

In his pocket full of treasures, he had whistles and jacks, gum wrapper, red string and three quarters. It felt good to have a pocket full of valuable stuff.

It was important to know what he should have in his pocket at any particular time. He didn't just grab random items before running out of the house in the morning. He had to be careful to chose well or the next thing the whole world would be in mortal danger. The simple solution could be the red string left home on the dresser.

Thank God, this had never happened. He knew he was calm, cautious and confident and always ready. He's chosen the right treasures every time.

~ Cynthia Babb Fry

If cats or children are acting a little crazy, they may be "galing for a storm," that is, predicting bad weather.

An Old Friend

Today I met an old friend
I had not seen in years.
She looked so young; I felt so old
I felt a shiver; my blood ran cold.

In years gone by,
We had so much to say
Of boys and dates and secret things
And when we might get those wedding rings.

The years have passed;
Nothing can last.
We all grow old
With aches and pains cramps and colds.

I pine for the days of long, long ago
When all my juices were not so slow.

~ G.M. Legge

To know who your future spouse will be, put a piece of wedding cake under your pillow and your dreams will show you the face of the one you will wed. This works especially well if you pass the cake through a wedding ring.

Uncle Joe

With a chaw of tobaccy tucked in his cheek,
His lopsided grin made me smile.
His blue eyes a'twinklin' and his hair white as snow,
That's how I remember him, my Uncle Joe.

He lived in an outport that's no longer there.
Now the hills only echo the wind.
There's no sound of people, no children at play,
No roosters to welcome the dawning of day.

Still the Sun rises and sets every day,
And the silent Moon crosses the sky.
Their life-giving energies cannot revive
The soul of a town that's no longer alive.

The Davidges, Hilliers, Fitzpatricks and Farrells
Once lived there in peace, all content.
If one needed help, everybody had time
And Mickey, the barber, cut hair for a dime.

I was still very young when I left there for good;
Now a half century's nearly gone by.
The memories I have of my life in that place
I'll cherish forever, no time can erase.

I remember at dawn how I'd jump out of bed
All eager to row up the brook
And help Uncle Joe saw lumber all day,
Get home at dusk, then go out and play,

With Gerald and David and Wally and Dick
And Harold and Bud and John Ben.
With a stick and a rock we'd play rounders till night
Then fall into bed wishing for more light.

I remember us young fellers thinking it smart
To hide and throw rocks at the girls,
And the day that Ron Lace, with his big friendly grin,
Shoved me over the wharf so I'd learn how to swim.

I remember the concerts and suppers we had
The accordion squeezing out tunes,
In the little white school house where I used to go,
Where Teacher Tom taught me the best that I know.

I remember the winters and sliding the hill
From the school down to Tommy Joe's cove.
I remember the very first money I earned
Selling tom-cods I jigged to the trader, Ches Yarn.

I remember the stories that Uncle Joe told
Of the years when he fished on the banks,
And the times that they had in the Lunenburg halls,
And his trek with Zane Grey to the big Smokey falls.

If I had the time I could sit and recall
Every moment I spent living there.
The weeds and wild grasses now cover its face.
It's vanishing slowly at nature's own pace.

Who would have thought that an outport could die,
And the codfish would someday be gone?
Now all that is left of that place I adored
Are the memories of my home, Bay du Nord.

What would I give to relive those years
To be young and carefree again,
Without any troubles or worries or fears?
Why, I'd give the rest of my life for
Just one day back then!

~ *Fred Stewart*
(1934 – 2007)

Diana

She married a real live Prince
And a Princess she became.
Too late she came to realize
That to him it was a game.

For he loved another,
And to Diana couldn't be true.
She didn't want to separate.
What else could she do?

She gave him two handsome Princes:
William and Harry by name.
That they couldn't remain a family
Was really a bit of a shame.

She was loved by all who met her
For her kind and gentle way.
She showed her care for everyone
Right up to her last day.

When she thought she'd be happy
After finding a wonderful man,
She had a tragic accident.
Terrible sadness fell over this land.

Now thousands line up by her home
And leave flowers and notes galore.
I hope Diana knows this
And has peace forever more.

~ *Florence Antle*

Stuart McLean

Good Bye, Old Friend.
I only got to say Hi
A few times.
Through your stories,
I got to know you.

You were an observer,
A listener who
Listened well.
You saw the little things
That most would overlook.

These things made up who we are.
Each week your voice
Filled our homes and cars.

You made us laugh and cry.
We knew you so well
That we would respond
Before you got to the next sentence.

You would stop,
Tell us not to get ahead of you
And continue on.

Now we have
To continue on
Without you, or
Dave or Morley.

Yet I smile.
You touched down in so
Many Canadian towns and cities.

I wonder, with all that great local music
You tuned us in to,
When they lay you to rest,
Will someone sneak
In a few lines of the
Flight of the Bumble Bee?

I think that would
Make you smile.

~ Jackie Sheppard Alcock

Did you hear about the lotto on the donkey? Hundreds of $5.00 tickets were sold, but before the winning ticket was drawn, the donkey dropped dead. The ticket seller was asked if anyone was upset that they'd bought tickets on a dead donkey.

"No," he replied. "No one except the winner cared. And I gave him back his $5.00."

The Piano

While browsing through my favorite classifieds, I spied an ad which read: *For Sale—Electronic Piano with Full Keyboard.*

Hmmm. It sounded very interesting. When I was a child we always had a piano in our home. We really didn't know music. Still, we played with it, so to speak. The piano seemed to be part of our furniture.

Years later, when my children were young, I purchased a second-hand piano for my own home. My daughters took lessons over the years and after a while, they became pretty good at rapping out a tune. I remember how sometimes they hated their lessons. The sudden abrupt banging on the keyboard demonstrated such emotions. They also marvelled at perfecting a piece of music. Occasionally. I would try my hand at it and found it very therapeutic.

My adult children moved on, but the piano remained in my house until I decided to change homes. The piano was left in my daughter's garage; it was too heavy to move ever again.

The time for pondering was over. It was time to make the call about the classified ad. This musical lightweight instrument would be a welcome addition to our new home. My husband and I asked for the civic address and we set off on our adventure.

The bungalow at our destination looked cosy, even if neglect had damaged its curb appeal and given it a sense of emptiness. I rang the doorbell and an elderly man followed by a taller, younger man invited us in.

I recognized the younger man from my mother's hospital room. Towering over her bed, he'd visited the lady in the bed across from us. He'd said, "I'll see you later, Mom," when he left after a short visit.

As we were going through the kitchen, the older gentleman said, "I spent 48 wonderful years with my Molly."

I felt his sadness, remembering him saying her name to his beautiful fragile wife in the cold hospital room. He'd turned on a soothing melody by Chopin before he left her bedside. A devastating stroke had confined her to that hospital bed. Her hands and long, slender fingers lay still. She was left totally dependent on others. Her eyes had followed me as I tended to my mother. Her husband had tried to bathe her in music to ease the sadness of her paralysis.

We walked through an empty room. "Molly taught her lessons here," he said.

Her son had always acted as if he couldn't wait to leave his mother's bedside. Was he an uncaring or heartbroken son who didn't care or was he shattered by his mother's illness? Silent and still, nothing without the dancing magic of her piano fingers.

Little did I know when we shared visits to our mothers in that dreary hospital room that I would be carrying Molly's piano up her steps and out her door to a different corner in a different room. It would bring joy to listening ears. I had listened to her music in the hospital and now I was taking it home with me.

We followed the son and his father downstairs to the basement. In a cluttered corner the piano sat amid boxes packed up, ready for a move. Sunbeams shone through the half-opened window shades and glistened on the black and white keys. Someone had taken the time to dust the piano. The instrument was immaculate and in perfect condition. I stepped over boxes in my way knowing instantly that the piano was mine.

When I told the gentleman that I wanted to purchase the piano, tears filled his eyes. He told us, "My wife used to be a music teacher. Her eyes lit up when her fingers hit the keys. She'd close her eyes, letting the music create a mesmerizing calmness, a peace for her and her family. This little corner of the rec room was her space, her world."

I thought of the pride parents must have felt as they watched and listened to their children making the piano talk while their teacher, Molly, stood proudly in the background applauding her students.

The younger man looked at his watch. "I'm sorry. I'm running late. I have to go now," he said. He hurried up the steps.

His father sighed as he watched his son leave without a backward glance.

We picked up the piano, stand, and plugs and carried them up the steps.

We rested when we reached the top of the stairs and talked. He had a worn, rugged handsome look. He ran his hand through his tufted hair. "I taught English at the University for years. Now I'm all alone, talking to you, perfect strangers, taking away Molly's music." He sighed. He seemed unware of the open fly in his pants. "I hope you enjoy the piano as much as my Molly did."

My heart went out to him as I said, "I'm sure I won't play as well as your Molly. My little granddaughters will enjoy playing it."

As we drove away he waved. His loneliness touched me. I imagined he missed intelligent conversation and companionship. Most of all he yearned for his Molly.

Basement treasures like Molly's piano hold stories of love, laughter, recitals and parties. How her fingers must have passionately danced over the keyboard, hypnotizing her students. With Molly as mentor, some students undoubtedly followed in her musical footsteps, bringing joy and wonder to their listeners.

Filled with emotions, I wondered if she had passed or if she remained confined to a slumberous state of existence. Some things seemed better unanswered. If life was simple, her fingers could be repaired as easily as a repairer could lift and fix a dropped key on her beloved piano.

The old professor seemed to yearn for their past; he ached for the scent of his cherished music teacher, his porcelain doll, partner and lover, broken, lying still with dormant fingers.

I turned to see him anxiously watching us. Another piece of her life, her piano, disappeared into the trunk of our car.

~ *Daisy Bennett-Lush*

Watch the Ashes Fall

Did you know it snowed on the day
You were born?
Soft white flakes drifted to the earth
As if God himself
Wanted to bless the special event
With manna from Heaven

Some dim-witted fool
In a bed nearby
Mocked me
Said it was ashes from Hell

Nothing was too good for my baby
Night and day I stood by your crib
Always there
To comfort you when you cried
You were all a mother could ask for

Oh my child!
It rained on the day you were buried
Crystal hard drops fell on
Your urn
They stayed for a moment
Then rolled like tears into the
Grey ground
That waited to enfold you
Ashes and earth
Have given birth to an unplanted
Flower
That grows white
Like the manna from Heaven

~ *Jean Legge Hiscock*

Cold Sensations

© *Victoria Young Kawaja*

Swimming Lesson

"Father, may I go swim today?"

"The wind's northeast and very cold
Enough to freeze the very soul.
No you can't go swim today."
Then he hove on his boots and went away.

With father gone he could not know
I disobeyed his orders so.
My friend and I climbed cliff and sand
And in the icy water swam,
Frolicking, screeching, having fun.
We did not heed the tides that come.
Lucky me I reached the shore
Breathless but breathing, that is sure.

My friend in the water is asleep
And she will all my secrets keep.
My tyrant father must not know
I disobeyed his orders so.

~ Jean Legge Hiscock

My Journey

The nurse pages my name to follow the red dots. My walking is labored. I can't keep up with her pace. She turns looking irritated because I'm so far behind.

"Are you coming?" she demands.

I mumble something about having trouble with my leg. She doesn't hear me. She's too far ahead.

Days prior, I pretended I knew what I was doing at Zumba. That night, my brain wasn't communicating with my leg. My leg had a brain of its own. Nope. Not moving! My thoughts were on saving face and getting off the dance floor. Afterward, my sister who had accompanied me asked, "What's up?"

I opened my mouth to speak. Only gibberish came out. No words would form.

Back up a few weeks.

I had been experiencing a cold sensation electrocuting one side of my face. I also noticed I was skipping a step while walking. This went on for weeks. Eventually it became more frequent. A year before, I was having hand tremors.

"Oh, you have anxiety, here's a pill for that," the doctor said.

"Take me to the hospital now!" Finally, my scared voice was requesting my husband to help me. I'd accepted it wasn't all in my mind. It took a stumble while cooking in the kitchen and a lucky save from falling into the hot stove to make me go.

I sit alone on a cold stretcher in Emergency. My husband has gone to park the car and I've been called in while he is gone. With no cell service I can't call or text him to come and he can't find me. My eyes hurt from the bleached white sheet. I want to cover up. I'm not given the luxury of a blanket. I shiver. The bed gets colder.

The doctor comes. He asks me a bunch of questions. "Do you think you know what's wrong?"

I reply with a guilty smile. "Well I've googled."

He confirms my Google search was probably accurate.

My thoughts turn to the goulash half-prepared on the stove at home. I should have put the meat in the refrigerator. A shame it's not stored properly. I wonder how it will be when I get home.

I am given instructions for examinations to come and dismissed. I stumble to the hallway. There's cell service here.

"Where are you?"

"I'm ready." I climb aboard the car in silence. How do I say this?. "Um.... aww...." Silence....

I'm home for lunch and notice a voicemail. Running late for work, I have no time to call. I rush back to the office. Take my place behind my desk. I pick up the phone and dial the familiar number.

"Can you come now? The doctor wants to speak to you."

It had been a year of symptoms. A year of "this is all in my head". It is. Literally. White spots they call lesions form a pattern called The Dawson's Finger. The doctor had confirmed the diagnosis of Multiple Sclerosis.

It's a mystery how one handles traumatic news.

In the five minutes my doctor shared with me, my life had officially changed. Yet all I could think of was hurrying back to work before they noticed me gone. I didn't call my husband who was also at work. Instead, I got into my car on autopilot and returned to the parking lot at work. I turned off the ignition and stared ahead.

My son had celebrated his 20th birthday two weeks earlier. Just the day before, I'd had my daughter's Sweet 16 birthday gathering. I was 36. Grateful now I'd had them young. It was meant to be.

The next month was a blur of appointments, treatment decisions, health insurance forms, and calls from the pharmaceutical company that wants my business. Google became my constant for research on the so many questions I had about my incurable chronic illness.

I tried to shield my family from worry. I'd spent the beginning days in denial. Retreating to my room one evening I couldn't keep my emotions together. This day was different. I was mad. So mad. Why me? Why now? Why? Why? Why!

The release that followed will never leave me. Gut wrenchingly mad, I sobbed until I had no more. Finally feeling done with the anger, I was now ready to embrace the acceptance.

I opened the room door only to realize my daughter had heard it all. Her body was shaking as she hid her face and tears in her pillow. Oh the guilt was all mine. I'd done this to her. I'd scared and hurt one of the people I wanted to protect the most.

That day, I vowed I would live my best life. This was not going to define me. I started attending physiotherapy rehabilitation to get strong and retrain my weakened limbs and muscles. I also planned my first real vacation away from home.

I am now in remission. This doesn't take away the symptoms or the unknown aspect of my future. Life is unpredictable at best for us all. I take no day for granted. This life I was given is MY journey. I will travel it however God decides.

Now on to the next Chapter....

~ Trina King

If a person has cold hands, she has a warm heart.

Hunger

Hunger in a world of plenty.
Thirst where all could drink their fill.
Why do we, our brothers' keepers,
Have the urge to maim and kill?

We see so much of thirst and hunger,
In commercials, on T.V.,
Will we share and ease their hunger
Or let them die in misery?

What to do when help is needed;
do we share and lend a hand?
Are we watchers and not doers
Or do we firmly take a stand?

We are blessed with gifts from nature,
From the land and from the sea.
What about our distant brothers
Who live in want and misery?

We come without technology,
And tell them how to live.
Is that what's really best for them
or what we want to give?

~ Nico LaBlanc
(Blanche Penney)
(1927 - 1989)

Reading Coffee Grounds

The family is eating breakfast.

The man's head lifts slightly to radio news:
"girl, eleven
found
was abducted
foster child
sold for sex. . . .

He straightens his tie
and the collar of his white shirt,
then lifts a mug to his lips,
meets its hot, muddy surface.
His daughter, eleven, tips
clear blue eyes to his.
He looks at her who knows only
the butterfly touch of a kiss on her cheek,
her fresh young face lifted with a question:
"What do these men do?"

"Men!" Her mother spits the word.
"These are not men, but animals."

The daughter draws back afraid,
and the man scrapes back his chair,
jumps startled, as if
he'd like to tear away
his clothes, his skin, his body
and run for his life.

~ Nellie P. Strowbridge

He Was My Nightmare

It all started June 19th
When I turned 6 years old.
He smacked me hard, so hard I cried.
Blood started trickling from my nose.

My mom came running to my aid.
He grabbed her and whipped her face.
She was crying and he got mad.
He ran somewhere and grabbed a knife.

He threatened to kill me and make her watch.
This made my mother scream with fear.
Then I saw something I never thought I'd see.
He stabbed my mother and down she fell.

I got up and ran through my house.
It seemed so unfamiliar now.
I wanted to find the phone
To call someone to help my mom.

I dialed 911
and gave a man my name and address.
I was just in time.
All of a sudden the line went dead.

He swore at me and I stared.
His clothes were bloodstained and torn.
I couldn't believe how this man had changed
From someone warm to a cold-hearted man.

Then I heard sounds which gave me hope,
sirens outside my house.
Four men burst in through the door,
threw my stepfather to his knees.

They cuffed him as he threatened me.
He said he'd kill me if he ever got out.
He killed my mother on this very day.
I was still shaking as they took him away.

It's four years later and I'm still in shock
I still have nightmares every night.
I think about it every minute
This horrible man who ruined my life.

~ Jennifer Sutton

A northeast wind brings no one any good

My Soul, My House

This is an excerpt from the interviews with Andrea Lees, resident of Deer Pond as reported by a journalist immediately before the explosion moved Deer Pond to White Bay.

(Solomon Gould is a gloomy sort to be around. I was volunteering at the Relay for Life Beer Tent and everyone had gone home besides Solomon. So I counted up the money, we did all right, too, paid for two more beers and me and him sat on the wooden bench and had a yarn.

Solomon thinks life owes him a living and therefore he is never going to work or do anything besides sell a bit of dope now and then to cover basic expenses and his own habit. Otherwise, he's going to wait for his big chance. He's not sure what the big chance he wants is; he expects it any day now. The only problem he sees is this "vision" he had last night when he was waiting for his kettle to boil.)

I was staring at the kitchen door and an angel, not your storybook kind, appeared. This angel showed up all in black, from the tips of his toes to the tips of his wings. He showed up smack dab in front of my face. I fell down on my knees. I was scared, man, I was scared.

"Arise, sinner and consider," the angel said. "Your house is like your soul. Doors hide Eternal Redemption, Endless Suffering, lives lived and yet to live. I see you wander through hallways seeking heavenly pearly gates, cold, jeweled streets, pure cool relief. You fear rusted iron bars, searing Hell fire, baptism. pure vigorous life. At each exit, you retreat."

"What are you talking about?" I asked when all I wanted was to get him out of my house.

"Live the way you do and you will find only the sameness and dullness of Limbo. Live more fully, experience all, discover the joys of behaving well. Begin now and you may be Redeemed."

I thought it over. I'd expected to go to Hell since I haven't done much good and while I haven't been all that bad, I do sell drugs to kids. He was saying I wasn't about to burn after all. And Heaven with cold, jeweled streets didn't sound all that hot. It sounded cold. I figures, if I keep on the way I'm going, I'm not doing all that bad so why change a good thing unless I gets my big chance. Then, I'll think about choosing a different way and I'll even set up a Rehab Centre for the kids I got hooked on dope.

So I thanked that black angel for his concern and told him to go see someone he might have a chance of influencing. You should have seen the look on his face! I thought I might have a bit of trouble getting rid of him, He caused no problems at all.

He whirled around in a little tornado and took off and he left a hole in the roof. The roof needed new shingles anyway.

~ *Deborah Hedd*

A call comes in at the 911 centre. "Me and my buddy was out hunting and his gun went off and I think he's dead!"

"Slow down. Take a couple deep breaths. The first thing we need to know for sure is, are you sure he's dead?"

"Wait a minute."

The 911 dispatchers hear a gunshot.

The caller comes back on the telephone. "Now I'm sure he's dead. What do we do now?"

A Silent Love

I wish that I could stop loving you.
I can't no more than I can stop
the wind from blowing or
the sun from shining or
the flowers from blooming in the spring.

Ours is a silent love.
A forbidden love.
A love that should never be.
But is.

It would be a shame to let this love pass us by.
It should be allowed to blossom and grow
Not wither away or die.
Thoughts of you make me happy,
so how can I say all is lost
when I can go back into my thoughts and
remember how you held me, and
said I will never forget you
No matter where you are?

A silent love
a forbidden love
a love that should never be.

~ *Terry Manuel*
(1961 - 2017)

Cold

I feel so old
My soul is cold
The sun is bright
Yet it feels like night
What can I try
So I'll not cry

~ Florence Antle

The Uncanny

The door closed quietly behind Ethel Hays, all alone in her isolated farm house. Her grown children had moved out and away to work in other towns.

After her husband, Alex, passed away, she had rented rooms to guests. Some had died over the years; others had gone back to their old homes near their families. She had the whole house to herself now.

As Ethel stood by the kitchen sink, she gazed out the window at the surrounding farmlands left to her and Alex by his parents. Barns needed a coat of paint, loose boards needed to be hammered in place, and the stable needed cleaning.

She had only one horse now, Kendra, her dappled grey mare, who was still up to a quick trot with Ethel astride. She willingly pulled Ethel's small buggy, too. Ethel wondered if Kendra missed Alex's horse. Captain, a prized, retired race horse, had died shortly after Alex passed away. Lately, Kendra seemed a mite fidgety when Ethel went to feed her.

Staring out through her window, thinking about Kendra, Ethel glimpsed a flash of white, an apparition, perhaps, near the old well, a very slight movement to the right of the handle. It wasn't the first time she'd sensed strange sights and sounds around the old farm. Who or what could that white flash be?

Ethel kept watching. Yes, she saw it again, the slight movement of flowing white material, a soft, flowing dress, perhaps. She squinted at a ghostly woman's figure gliding along, floating towards the back door of the stable, her movements refined and elegant.

Leaning toward the window pane, Ethel wondered what the ghostly woman was up to. She never looked at Ethel, at the house, not at all. Had she lived here at the farm before Alex's parents moved in? Alex's mother had been tall and heavy.

Ethel always had a little too much curiosity, and that often led her into tricky situations. Alex had tempered her eagerness with advice and a warning to be careful before dashing into danger.

The woman disappeared. Ethel walked to the back door, tempted to go to the well, to see if the woman was more than a ghost. She felt Alex saying, "Be careful, Ethel. You can wait until morning. You mustn't go out all alone in the dark."

She wasn't afraid of the dead. Still, the feeling of apprehension warned her not to follow the ghostly figure.

"Fine, Alex. I'll wait until daylight." Ethel often found herself speaking to Alex as if he were still around. She took a deep breath and decided to stay in for the night. She was a sixty-six-year-old woman living alone on a farm, with no close neighbours. The figure could be a vagrant or someone trying to get her out of the house for some nefarious reason.

Thinking about the strange figure, Ethel remembered the talented magician who had stayed with her as a guest. He'd been a master at creating illusions, making unreal objects appear in her line of vision.

Ethel wondered if he had a female assistant. It was too dark to get a good look at the apparition. She waited, watching to see if the woman would appear again, closer to the house. The farmyard stayed silent and empty of the ghostly figure. Ethel closed her curtains and turned off the kitchen lights. Let any creatures of the night stay outside in the dark.

She prepared a late supper, put it on her tray, and carried it into her living room. She sat down on the ancient chesterfield and turned on the television to watch her favorite show, *Little House On the Prairie*.

When Ethel's show was over, she thought about the times she and Alex sat next to each other, talking about what had happened that day. Alex was no longer with her. She did not want to talk to herself.

When Ethel stood up to turn off the television, she heard a quiet voice. She shivered in surprise, stopped moving and listened. She struggled to hear more clearly. Yes, the soft whispery voice came again.

"Henry, where are you?"

Henry, the name of the magician! Why would the whispery voice call out to Henry? Henry had left months ago.

As the voice faded, Ethel thought back to the other strange happenings after Alex's death. Things had disappeared from the house, items that were only significant to herself and Alex. She often heard voices in the night; some seemed to come from the attic. She refused to believe she was becoming demented. When a person is living alone, looking after the farm herself, without any close family and friends, hearing voices would naturally make her feel afraid and unsure of herself. Who would offer her guidance and comfort?

And yet, she thought, why after all this time since Alex's death, am I hearing a whispery voice and seeing a ghostly woman? Ethel was never one to back down from a challenge. Come daylight, she was going to investigate down by the stable.

First on the agenda: a good night's sleep, and then she'd tackle the questions in the morning. Ethel checked all of the doors and the windows, making sure everything was locked up tight. Then she headed for the servants' quarters where she'd slept since Alex death. The memories didn't hurt so much away from her old bedroom.

Ethel stood still outside her bedroom door for a minute, to see if she could hear the whispery voice. All was silent except for her own breathing. She entered the room, quickly undressed for bed and slipped under the covers. Despite her uneasiness, she fell into a deep sleep and didn't see or hear anything until the sun shone through the curtains the next morning.

The alarm clock chimed eight times before she shut it off. "Time to get up," she mumbled. She slowly rose from the bed, entered her bathroom, washed and dressed and headed for the kitchen to make some breakfast.

While cooking a couple of eggs, Ethel thought about the previous day. Why were all the mysterious things happening on the farm? Should she do her own investigation, to find out if the ghostly woman was real, if she was whispering to Henry. And why the heck was Kendra so edgy?

Finishing her breakfast, she headed for the sink to wash her dishes. As she rinsed her plate off, someone knocked on the door.

Grabbing Alex's rifle, she tiptoed to the door. The lightly-frosted glass window of the back door, showed a silhouette of a man.

She called out, "Who are you?"

"It's Kent."

Thank heavens! She recognized the voice of her oldest son,

"Mother, may I come in?" asked Kent. "What's with the rifle?"

"Oh yes, sorry about that. I was surprised to hear a knock on the door and to see you standing outside," said Ethel.

"Well, I'm not the only one you are going to see," said Kent.

"What do you mean?" Ethel asked.

"Dawn, Darius, and Kaitlyn should be arriving soon. We've been keeping in touch since we moved away," said Kent. "I won't explain any further until my brother and sisters get here. Then we won't have to speak three times more."

"Have you had breakfast, son?" Ethel asked.

"No, and I don't think the others have either," Kent replied.

"I'll make some breakfast for you all, like old times", said Ethel.

She turned and was about to get the eggs, when she heard another knock on the door.

When Kent answered it, Ethel's three other children rushed in and gave her bear hugs and kisses.

When the excitement died down, Dawn looked at her mother and said, "Mother, we've been worried about you; we had to come home."

"Now, now, my dears, everything is okay now that you're all home. Nothing in this world can make me happier, I believe once you have eaten your breakfast you can tell me, what you're so worried about."

The chatter was light-hearted as breakfast was eaten and dishes were rinsed and put into the sudsy dishwater.

Kent, the eldest, began the conversation.

"Mother, we all loved you and Dad very much, and we loved this farm. With the weird noises and ghostly apparitions, it bothered us so much we couldn't sleep."

"That's why we moved away. We all keep in touch because we are worried about you, Mom," Darius said.

"I am concerned about the voices I've heard lately," Ethel admitted. "They sound very familiar, but the ghost doesn't make any sound. It hovers quietly around the stable every evening."

"Mother", Dawn added, "we've all been scared of the ghost."

"My darlings, the dead won't hurt you, it's the living you must watch out for," Ethel said. "I think we may have live intruders on the farm. That makes me nervous."

"I think we must arm ourselves for protection against whoever is out watching us, then. We'll wait until this evening and try to catch the intruders. We must not let them know we're here. We'd better hide our cars," Darius said.

"Follow me," Ethel said. "The shed behind the house should be big enough."

They drove the cars into the shed and chatted the day away until late afternoon. They went to the stable with their mother. As they drew near the stable doors, they heard Kendra stamping her feet and neighing. Someone had tied her up outside her stall.

Ethel shook her shoulders in an irritated gesture, "Who put Kendra out of the stall? Look at the floorboards. They've all been pried up," she said angrily.

"Mother, the floor in Captain's old stall is pried up too," Kent said.

Ethel patted Kendra, soothing her. She filled her water bucket and her manger. "There, there, my girl. You'll be fine. I'll put you in one of the other stalls for tonight." She turned to her children. "Let's go to the house and keep watch."

When they entered the house, Ethel noticed a flowery smell. "Does anyone smell lavender?" she asked

Her children nodded yes. Kaitlyn said, "It seems to be very strong by the bottom of the bannister that goes upstairs."

"I know I locked the door. I always do, even if I'm only going for eggs." Ethel said.

"We know Mother, but someone was in this house; they must have seen us going into the stable, and decided that was a good time to look for something in the house," Dawn said.

"These are not the actions of a ghost. I think we have two people searching for something," Kent surmised. "We'll stay together and search the house, top to bottom."

They looked into every room, under the beds, in the closets, in the attic and down in the cellar. Nothing moved and they saw no sign of anyone, alive or dead.

"The house is all clear. We'll wait until dark and turn the lights out. Let the intruders think we are all asleep." Kent gave the orders and no one argued.

They turned out the lights and everyone sat in the corner of the kitchen and waited. After an hour or so, Ethel said, "Listen! Do you hear that?"

"Shh," Kaitlyn spoke softly.

From the hallway near the stairs, a whispery female voice floated in.

"Ohh, Henry, where are you? Where are you Henry?"

A male voice responded, "Shhh, keep quiet; don't wake the old woman."

"I'll old woman him," Ethel grumbled. "I know that voice; it's the magician Henry."

"What was that noise, Henry? It's the ghost. I know it's the ghost. I want to leave."

"Cut it out! Ethel's asleep and you know the ghost is not real," said a male.

"Well I know I saw a ghost," the female answered softly.

"Well, if we can't find it, we have no choice. We'll make the old woman talk, ghost or no ghost," the male growled.

Ethel gasped as she looked at her family. She whispered, "What are they talking about?"

"What was that noise, Henry?"

"That's it Terri, enough of this ghostly stuff; where did you look?" Henry demanded.

Under the horse's stalls, in the attic, the basement, etcetera, etcetera, etcetera."

"Why would you look in those places Terri? It's a diamond not a blasted watermelon," Henry complained.

Kent looked at his mother and whispered, "I'm calling the law." He eased out the door to make the call as footsteps moved up the stairway to the room Ethel had shared with Alex.

The Sheriff and his Deputy left their car sheltered behind trees and came quietly up the long driveway. Ethel and her children pointed to the stairway.

Henry and his partner were grumbling as they came down the stairway. Henry said, "She's not in her room. It doesn't look as if she's slept in that room for ages. You should have noticed that."

"Henry, you always get me to do the dirty work. I never get to saw you in two or throw knives at you. I had to search this house and stay quiet as a mouse. Now you finally show up. You don't say, 'thank you, Dee, for doing all that searching.' No, all you do is complain."

They came to a full stop - staring at Sheriff Dumont and Deputy Sharp standing at the bottom of the staircase with their guns drawn.

Sheriff Dumont ordered them: "Put your hands up and come down, slowly, very slowly."

Deputy Sharp handcuffed the two; then he tipped his hat at the Hays family. "We'll be in touch in the morning." The two thieves were marched down the long lane.

After they left, Kent went to lock the door. He took one last look around before closing up for the night. He saw the ghostly woman crooking her finger, as if to say, "Follow me."

"Mother, look she wants us to follow her," Kent said.

"Let's go." Ethel pushed past Kent and her children followed her and the ghostly woman through the orchard.

The woman, dressed in a flowing white gown, fading in and out of their sight, stopped at a gnarly old apple tree. She pointed to a hole big enough for a fist to fit in.

Darius reached inside and pulled out a small wooden box. Inside the box, the most beautiful diamond lay nestled in red velvet on a small white paper note. He passed the box to his mother.

She picked up the note and she read "*To My Beloved Ethel, All my love, Alex.*"

As Ethel looked up, she saw the ghost lady smile. Right beside the unknown spirit, Ethel's husband, Alex, riding Captain, appeared. Alex blew her a final kiss and the three ghosts faded away.

The family turned to one another, each wondering who the ghostly lady was and how she'd found a way to make Ethel's financial worries go away.

One of the farm's mysteries was solved. Others remained.

~ *Norma Jean House*

Telling ghost stories may bring on a storm.

"Exhausted"

Found wherever I go.
Hunted by sweat.
Poured out till only drops remain.
Sometimes I think
it's just to test how much is in me.
Used until emptiness sets in
to solve someone else's problem.

Drank by other people,
abandoned when depleted.
A tool, useful when strong,
discarded when broken,
ignored when unnecessary.

Not really a person;
politeness and my name
are afterthoughts on their lips.
To them I have nothing to say except
whether or not I can do what they ask.
And by ask I mean demand.
'No' not truly an option in their minds.

Too busy to start something for myself;
too tired to deal with the explosion
that would happen if I said no.
Too tired to keep going,
too tired to stop.
What can I do?

~ Jamie Stuckless

Not A Bedtime Story
1984

Jolene always pinned a diaper on Jay, her year-old baby, with meticulous care. She slipped one hand on the inside of the diaper she was pinning. Otherwise, any movement and the pin could pierce his soft, white skin. She'd seen it happen with other babies as their mothers hurried to diaper a squirming child. If anyone was going to feel the prick of a diaper pin it would be her.

She tucked her baby's blue blanket around him and sat his large teddy bear in the corner of the crib so he could see it when he awoke. Then she sat by the crib until he closed his bright brown eyes.

He always fell asleep quietly, breathing gently, a tiny smile on his lips. He never made a murmur of discontent. Pride rose like a soft lump in her throat. Having her boy was her ultimate triumph after years of trying. Thinking this, she tiptoed out of his room, closing the door gently. Jay would sleep through the night, awake with a smile and babble to his teddy bear, something he did every morning.

Had she even suspected the possibility of what could happen in the next while, she might have tucked a few soft cookies and an extra bottle of milk into her baby's crib when she'd kissed him good night. Her hugs would have been longer.

She sat in her living room sewing buttons on a jacket she had made for her baby. She could see her boy in it. The soft earth tone jacket would match his brown eyes and brown hair, his unblemished porcelain skin emphasized. She laid the finished jacket aside, turned off the light and walked through the hall. She passed her son's room and went into her own bedroom where she planned on reading *Below the Bridge* by Helen Porter. All was quiet. She missed her salesman husband. Jace would be home from a business trip on Saturday. Five more days.

She washed her face and hands in the bathroom sink and rubbed cold cream into her skin. Then she came out and reached to turn on the light in the boudoir lamp beside her bed. She loved her lamp. Its blue glow was soft and romantic. She wished her husband was home.

It was almost dark and she reached her hand up, forgetting she had taken out the blown bulb. She had forgotten to buy another one when she went to the store that afternoon. Her hand, wet from the cold cream, slipped into the empty socket. Her body jittered, waves of shock passing through her.

"She was shocked to death," her husband would say later, "and I wasn't home." It was really a weak heart. Jolene had risked her own life to bring Jay to term. Her enlarged, weak heart had pulsed above Jay's tiny heart before his birth and had stayed strong throughout his delivery, strong enough for her to care for her son until now.

Jay woke the next morning and smiled at his teddy bear. Then he pulled himself up to the rails and babbled sounds his mother always heard and understood. He watched the door and waited, babbling, "Mom, Mom." He stopped as if he was listening for footsteps and expecting to see his mother coming to lift him from his crib. He was already wrinkling his nose at the unpleasant odor emanating from his diaper.

"Ur-ur!" he called.

Jay's face took on a troubled expression. He was used to his mother grabbing him up with a smile and a laugh. She would bring him into the bathroom to the change table to be bathed, rubbed with Johnson's baby powder and dressed. He plopped down and pulled his teddy bear into his arms. Then he stood up and called, "Momma!" He sucked his lips in and gnawed on them, his gums tightening as if there should be something tasty in his mouth.

Finally, his face strained, his lips fell open and he let out a pitiful cry. He kept his eyes on the door. Then he let out an anguished wail.

The baby's room was at the end of the house near a furniture store. The manager heard the cry, and the wails that followed. He looked towards the curtained window of the nursery, shook his head and grumbled, "Time for that mother to get herself out of bed and tend to her youngster."

Later that day, he heard the child again, this time a mournful, sobbing cry. "Probably watching the soap operas," he muttered, scarcely paying attention, a minor noise against the scraping of furniture being pulled from the back of his truck. He was in business and minding his own business was what he was doing.

The mother's sister called and, after several rings, hung up. She assumed that her sister was out with the baby.

The ringing of the telephone had awakened little Jay who, exhausted, had fallen asleep. He cried again, plaintive cries and sobs that tore through his body, racking it with pain. He felt the silence and aloneness and hunger even though he didn't understand any of it. His diaper, heavy with urine and feces, was hanging off his dirty bum. His momma always made him feel so happy. Now he had lost her. He tried to pull himself up and over the crib rails.

His grandparents, who lived less than sixty miles away, would have come, had they known. Instead, they went about their days ignorant of their daughter's fate and their grandson's peril. A sister-in-law thought of phoning the next day; she put it off to go shopping.

Lassitude set in and the baby settled into a fetal position. He had pulled off his diaper and thrown it over the rail. Now flies buzzed around it, some pitching on the drying feces.

Next door neighbours left their home for work and returned. Nighttime, they glanced once in a while at the house. There were no lights so they assumed that the mother and child had gone away. The cat, left outside, made loud, mewling sounds, and still no one thought to check on the mother.

Jay's lachrymose cries lessened and he fell in and out of sleep. Only his eyes moved as if he was searching for the face of the mother who would hold him and comfort him. His lids, with their soft, golden lashes, fell over his eyes like curtains closed to keep out the night. His quietness blended with the stillness of the house. With all the world around him, he was alone.

Jace pulled into the driveway on Saturday. The cat had thrown up on the doorstep and was sitting to one side meowing. Jolene had not answered the phone the couple of times he had called, so he had assumed she had taken the bus to her mother's for a few days.

He tried the door, frowned, and then pushed in his key. Jolene should be home. She knew he was hoping to be back today. His annoyance disappeared when he got inside and sensed the dead silence and an unfamiliar scent mingling with a familiar one. He raced into the hall, reaching his son's bedroom first. Weeping uncontrollably, Jace grabbed the still child to his chest, his arms hanging like a ragdoll's. The baby stayed inert, and, holding him, he rushed to his own room and dropped to his knees at the sight of his dead wife.

The child stirred slightly as the father's tears fell on his face. A shudder went through his little body and the father rushed to dial 911.

~ *Nellie P. Strowbridge*

This story was written in the days when mothers still pinned diapers with safety pins and used baby powder.

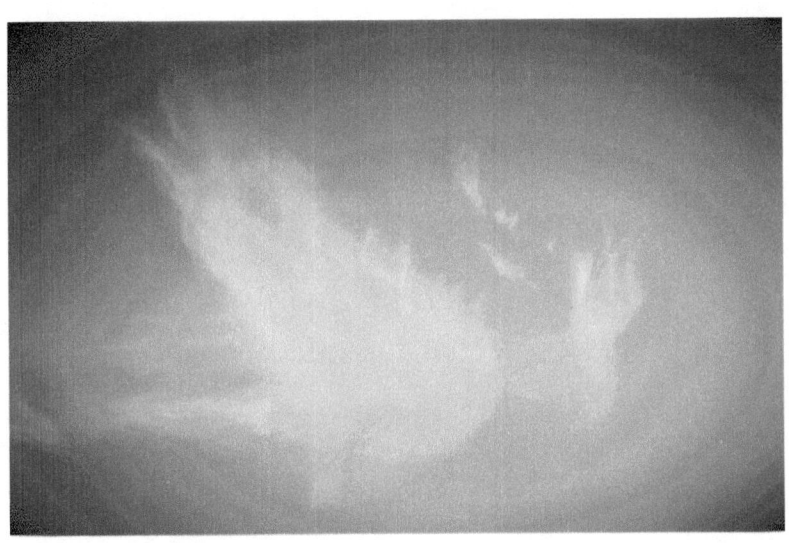

Feed My Addiction

I gotta feed my addiction
feed my pain
up my nose, in my veins.
I gotta have money to feed my addiction.

I break out in a sweat
desperate don't you see.
This demon has to be fed.

All my dreams go up in smoke
hard-earned money
down the drain.
Nobody gets paid except my addiction.

~ Francis King

"He smokes like a tilt."
   A tilt is the name given to a rough shack built by woodsmen to provide shelter. The makeshift stove tended to smoke up the whole tilt.

Dear Sis

I haven't emailed you for a while. I've been a little put out by what you said about Clint. I wouldn't say anything like that about your son, if you had one. I have to tell you about my day in court – well more than one day. We've been at this on and off for more than two years. I know you think we can't afford a lawyer: me and the old fella working part-time. It's not the way it used to be, us losing the house after he drank too much and we had to move to the basement of Mother's house.

I know you thought Katie, my ex-daughter-in-law, was sweet and kind and remembered my birthday and the old fella's birthday, among other things, something our son never did. I'll miss that.

She had some nerve to tell him she was leaving the marriage and taking the youngsters after she came home and caught him under a truck he was repairing while the boys, then two and five, were in the house, the youngest one up on the table. He's a climber, that one. Even then, he was smart enough to know how to slide down on a chair without falling.

Marriage is about communicating. Katie should have talked to Clint about leaving the children alone. Well, maybe she did a few times. Some men got to be told over and over, though Clint never wanted to be told anything. He sure didn't like it when she told him off for shooting a squirrel in the house in front of the boys and laughing at the gory mess. "That'll teach it not to take over my property," he said.

Katie expected my son to stay in the house with the youngsters while she was at work. Anyone knows he wanted to be outside fixing up old vehicles and selling them to put money in a bank account she knew nothing about. I was right in telling Clint he should have his own account. You never know what can happen to a marriage. He opened a joint account with my first name, his first name and my maiden name. After all, he was mine before he was hers. She need not think otherwise. Oh yes, he had to have something for himself. What's he living for? You know men. Still, they had to scrimp to make it on Katie's salary. The company's too mingy to give her overtime.

One morning the other grandmother showed up and took the boys to her place after Katie complained that she was worried about them. Clint only scrubbed the older youngster's head with his knuckles to toughen him up so that when he went to school he could handle the bullies. The other grandmother told Clint that if he kept it up, his son would be the bully. He let her take the children only because he didn't want her to report him, not with that other stuff on record when he was a teenager and knew no better.

Katie shouldn't have gone to work, she with two youngsters. If she'd kept after Clint, he would have come to his senses and got a steady job. He worked long enough to get his stamps for EI. He lengthened his claim by signing up for school and putting in for babysitting money. He kept that for himself. He had a good thing going. Whenever he didn't want to go to school he'd go see a doctor. Before doctors got too modern with the computer, he could get hold of their prescription pads. He bragged about slipping a slip from under his doctor's nose and writing himself a sick note. The things he can get away! He's smart.

I know Clint should have paid more attention to the youngsters instead of having his nose in the computer or out in the yard under an old truck he bought to fix up and sell. He's only trying to make a bit of extra money for himself. Every young fellow needs that. I told him he shouldn't leave the boys alone. He could bring them down to me or have Katie's mother babysit. We did often enough and never took a cent of babysitting money. He wanted time for himself something he got enough of. You couldn't tell him that. He'd get mad or all defensive.

I suppose I couldn't blame Katie for checking up on the boys while she was working. She'd phone and get them on the phone whenever he'd let them talk to her. He had to lay down the law and make her understand that he'd only look after the boys during the day until 5:30. Then his shift was over; it was her turn. As soon as she got in the door every evening she had to take over and make the dinner and whatever. It's what we did in our generation. Men haven't changed. Sure, he learned from his father.

Anyway, I told you that I work part-time where Katie works. She got me the job after I lost the one at the shoe store. I came upon her laughing and yapping with the girl who worked the phones in the office and a security guard: both of them unmarried. She shouldn't be talking to unmarried people and my son home minding the boys. Sure, I saw her smiling and chatting as if she knew them all. The engineers and security people took to her because she's what I call flirty and she calls being friendly.

Only once I phoned her mother and told her that Katie shouldn't be so friendly with the people who work in this building, a lot of single people here and she, a married woman carrying on. Stacey upstairs is not married. Now what do they have to talk about? Katie is acting as if she's a single woman, sure enough.

Katie's mother didn't want to hear any of it. She told me to look after my own affairs. What affairs? I've never had affairs. That's the old fella's department. I wish I'd had someone to keep an eye on my man when he was running around.

My son is the jealous type, and with that red hair, you know the combination. When Katie started working, he didn't want her wearing lipstick. She stopped wearing it after he smeared it across her face. He came down to the office one day after I'd told him a few things. She was upstairs on her break. When he saw her talking and laughing with the other workers he yelled at her to get the hell back down to the office. When she asked where the boys were he told her to never mind.

I don't think he ever struck her, not even at home, though some husbands would have. I understand why he was so mad. Here she was laughing and joking at work. She hardly smiled when she was with him in the last months they were together.

Clint bought Katie a cell phone for Christmas the year before she left. He made one payment on it and left the rest for her to pay out. Sure, she's the one working. He phoned her whenever he wanted to, especially if she wasn't home on the dot. Going to the grocery store after work was not an excuse. She and her mother blamed me for making Clint so jealous. I had nothing to do with it. I stayed out of their lives. I told the judge that.

Clint spread a story that she was having an affair with the security guard. He told her if she wasn't having one, she was having one in her mind. The security guard found out and threatened to punch him out. Clint told him, "No harm, Man. I was only trying to get a rise out of her."

He told Katie's mother that if Katie didn't quit her job he was going to go down and blow the place up. Her mother asked him if he was serious and he said he was. That's when she called the manager and told him. Meddling she was. Clint wouldn't do that. All talk! It was her fault that he wasn't allowed in the building after that.

Katie seemed to be on edge with Clint the last going off. So what if my son poured a cup of hot water down the back of her neck. It's not as if she was naked. She was wearing a sweater and she pulled away the minute the water touched her back. Most of it ended up on the chesterfield. I was only making a joke when I said, "Be thankful, he gave you a glass of water. Not every man will bring his wife a glass of water and pour it too."

She's got no sense of humour, that one. These things happen. Get over it! No one's perfect. He got a temper. The knife he left in the wall was only for show.

After she said she was leaving and taking the youngsters, he fixed her by making the first move. When she got home after work on a Friday evening she found a suitcase on the veranda and the locks on the doors changed. You should have seen her face. I saw hers; she didn't see mine. I was looking through a side window. Clint had stuffed a few articles of clothes, along with an old toothbrush she used to scrub the faucets in the bathroom sink, into an old suitcase.

It's not as if she had no place to go. Her mother lives only a few miles away. The boys bawled for their mother so I gave them candy and some Benadryl. That sure quieted them. Their little heads were lolling all over the place.

Katie got back into the house through the basement door the next morning. Clint had forgotten to change that lock. She came only for the youngsters. She's too attached to them. At night she would sit in the rocking chair reading to them. Clint didn't break the chair and put holes in the wall. The boys did that with their toys. She should have had Clint read the boys a bedtime story. No, she was lying on the bed, after the chair got broken, reading stories and laughing with the boys. Clint fixed that when she said she was leaving. He wouldn't let her near them to read a story that first week. He did it all. He was some father. What a change! He doesn't call himself The Riddler for nothing. She should have given him a chance.

Clint wanted her to stay home and look after the boys. He even said he shouldn't have forced her into getting her tubes tied, that if they had another child she would have to stay home and look after the youngsters, because he damn well wouldn't. He'd had his turn. She agreed to have her tubes tied after he threatened to leave her when she was pregnant with the second child. While she was under the knife having our youngest grandchild and groggy from the anesthetic he was firm on what he wanted. He didn't want the surgeon to be shy. He told him to cut her tubes and burn them, too. The surgeon thought she was nodding yes. I think he burned them.

Katie was quiet around Clint the last goin' off; something was bothering her. She didn't talk about it. It was on her affidavits in court, something shockin' the things she said about Clint, and he my son. He wasn't perfect, but you know it's enlarged on.

The judge didn't say anything about Clint not looking after the boys. Sure that's men. It doesn't come to them naturally. I got one here.

I don't think the judge believed anything she told him. He gave an interim order for her and Clint to have alternate weeks with the boys. That worked with my help and the other grandmother's all summer. Well, there were a few instances before Clint took off to Toronto to look for a job, leaving me to take up his slack.

Clint was so far away he couldn't show up for the court hearings. I kept putting in affidavits on his behalf trying to get him to apply for full custody. He could take the boys to the mainland with him. He was a bit saucy. He told me I'm not interfering in his life, now that he has an immigrant girlfriend. Fiancée, excuse me. He said, he's moving on.

"Sure," he says, "if you pull out your kids' pictures, whoever you're with will think you got baggage." My son is having none of that. He's thinking he might have youngsters with his new Mexican woman. I'm thinking she's already pregnant. Clint said he could see the kids when he brings his fiancée home. I put the boys on the phone with their father when they are here and whenever I can track him down. That's good. I don't want them to forget him.

The judge didn't want to go back to the past. "That has no relevance now," he said. The wall that Katie says Clint put the rocking chair through has been plastered. The other grandfather fixed the chair so that the mother can rock the youngsters in it, even if the legs are shorter. What odds that Clint and I forged Katie's name to buy a car for him to go away in. Then he told everyone she was in debt up to her eyeballs. He said he could do anything with a signature and he can. No lies about it. Sure, none of that is relevant now, nor that he hid his truck and stole the car she drove to work. She couldn't do anything about that. It was registered to him. When she thought she was being videotaped outside her mother's house – she was. Clint was only trying to get some evidence on her.

I made an application to the court for two and a half hours a week with the boys. I was being generous in only asking for that much. I had the boys a lot more than that when Clint was home.

The judge said we were very loving grandparents, and he saw no reason not to give us access. I'm sure he would have given us more time if we had asked for it.

Katie had a nerve to put in an affidavit that she noticed signs of regression after each visit at my house. The oldest boy went home to her mother's house and pooped in the toilet brush holder. He cut a hole in the chesterfield and he peed in a desk drawer – at different times, mind you. The brat was just being mischievous. Either that or he missed his father. I'm not giving her his address. Sure, she'll go after him for child support. First when they broke up, he tried to get spousal support. That didn't happen. It's too bad he's away. He ran himself out of jobs here. Anyway, he'll never pay child support. He'll work under the table.

I don't know why the judge couldn't wear a nice pair of black pants and white shirt instead of that dress – gown. Whatever! That's how it is. It's a wonder he doesn't don a powdered wig. He looks like a judge from the last century.

Well, maid, I got such a dose of diarrhea I got to run before it goes right down through me. You've heard me say that often enough. Nerves, I s'pose.

I'm back now.

It's great that the judge made an order that I pick up the boys at the other grandmother's house without even consulting her to see if his order would interfere with her time. She has to be home for me to pick them up whether she wants to be or not. Serves her right for squealing on my son. The judge wouldn't even allow her affidavit to be filed in court.

Access to the two boys for two and a half hours a week is enough for me. My bones are brittle and could crack any minute. I wouldn't want that to happen while I'm around the youngsters. I might have to go to Outpatients. They're used to me. I hardly have to take a number. As for the old fella, he's been ready to have a heart attack for years. His cholesterol's gone through the roof, so he's not keen on the stress of grandchildren. I hope the mother doesn't remember him calling them "the lousy kids" and saying they could come to visit, but they couldn't stay. She'll have it in a court document, though I know, for sure, that the judge won't believe her. His wife is friends with my sister and he coaches a basketball team my niece is on. He asked Katie if he needed to excuse himself from the case. I could see she was afraid to say yes for fear he'd hold it against her. She'd never been to court before the separation. Not like my son.

I've told you all I did for the boys. The oldest one enjoyed playing games. He'd poke me in the breast until it was sore. Other times, he'd stick out his tongue and I'd touch it with mine. His mother saw it happen once and called it lizard kissing. She said she didn't want it to happen again. In court she made it sound dirty. If that wasn't insulting enough, she testified that before she and Clint separated I was always claiming the oldest boy was sick and that I was giving him medicine when he didn't need it. I know he had an infection. He was running to the bathroom every few minutes. She said he stopped doing that once he was at Transition House. She brought a note to court from the doctor saying the child did not have penile cystitis. When I gave the children medicine for a cold she called it doping them up and when I used suppositories to keep them regular, she got upset over that. She complained that I gave them baths during my access and let them run around in their underwear. Then when they went to her mother's house they stripped off and wrapped themselves in a blanket and hid in the closet. Katie told the court that when she tried to bathe them after they were at my house they got agitated and whiny. The oldest one told her his bird hurt and Gramma put cream on it. The foreskin was tight, same as Clint's at that age. I had to pull it back to loosen it, too, even though he cried. I put cream on the boys when they complained of being sore. It was all innocent.

The oldest boy told her a lie. It's not true that I use my bare hands to wash the boys when they're in my bathtub. When I told the oldest boy he could only love me – no one else, I was joking. He shouldn't have taken me seriously and told his mother. Well anyway, that mother – the minute the youngest grandson complained that his grandfather hit him with his belt during our court-ordered visit, she refused us our right to our own grandchildren unless the visit was supervised. Well, you should have seen me in court. I tell you, I showed the judge I could cry, and my other half, sure he even wiped his eyes. No tears, he wiped his eyes anyway. Who does she think she is? We'd both give our livers and lights for them children – as least I would.

She got Child Protection Services on our backs. Anyone knows children can't be believed – seen and not heard – that was the way when I was a child, no matter what went on in the family. What do these young social workers know? The social worker said that the child told her, "I hate it when Gramma's Poppy hits me with his belt." Then he put his hands over his eyes and said he wanted to go asleep. You and I know that in our day, it was nothing to spank a child with a belt when it was justified. My lawyer tripped up the social worker, took a good strip off her. Sure, she didn't know if she was coming or going by the time she sat down. That will teach her to not listen to the boys mouthing off about us. My grandson had the colour of the belt wrong. It was not black. I had a picture to show that the old fella only wears a brown belt. So that was good.

My dear, you should have seen Katie's face when the judge ordered her to allow us to have the children during our allotted time. She had a Legal Aid lawyer who, if he was any quieter, he'd be dead. After 27 years in the business, maybe he figures he has a right to take a nap during court. Sure the judge asked him a question one time and he was so long in answering, my lawyer answered for him. She got a mouth on her like a bullhorn, couldn't stop talking, and the other lawyer couldn't start. It worked well for me. My other half heard the mother say something to her lawyer outside the court about being willing to go to jail rather than follow the court order. Sure, his face almost broke out of its skin. He sputtered, his lips pushed out like something hemorrhoidal, if you get my drift.

When Katie still refused access, we managed to get in a contempt charge and request that she pay all the court charges. See, it's not right for her to have so much control over our grandsons.

The judge had allowed Clint the right to serve an application for a contempt order. He wasn't interested so I did it in his name. According to the rule, a contempt order is supposed to be served on the person to be committed within twenty days from the date the order is granted. The time to do that ran out and when the judge told my lawyer in court that he couldn't go ahead with the contempt charge because of a rule of law, my lawyer, bless her heart, assured him, "Unless a judge otherwise orders it. My Lord, you can order it," she told him – and he did.

In the Interim Order made by another judge when this judge was not available, our access for two and a half hours a week was in effect only for so long; then we had to make another application to the court. Katie, not her lawyer mind you, told the court that no continuation of that order had been made. So when the contempt hearing was held, they had no court order allowing our access. We hadn't put in an application. As you can see, we didn't need to.

We had two days in court with Katie on trial and claiming she had no malice intent. She was trying to protect her boys. Doesn't she

73

know that's what courts are for? She had it in for us because we were Clint's parents. She claimed that her rights to protect the children should come above the rights of a grandmother who has shown contempt for their mother's rights, that grandparents' rights should be at the discretion of the parent committed to raising the children. The judge warned her that if she didn't allow the access awarded us he would send her to jail. He said he wouldn't want to, but if that's what it took to make her listen he would. Good enough for her. She'd lose her job and get a criminal record.

The Honourable Judge said, "I've been practicing for fifteen years."

I can hear her now: *You've been practicing for fifteen years. When do you expect to get it right?*

"And my gut tells me this is one parent trying to get one up on the other. You will probably be the custodial parent of those children; it worries me if they are being parented by someone who has a really strange view of the relationship these children should have with their father and, as well, with their paternal grandparents."

That Turner woman, the doctor, who was in the news for killing the father of her baby did us grandmothers a favour, especially after she walked into the water with her baby. Well, I don't mean she had to kill herself and baby Zachery. Still, in the end it was one bad turn that made a good one. Grandparents have more rights.

The judge said, "It looks as if you're the best parent at the moment. I understand the father is away."

I can still see her draw in a deep breath. It was if the judge was saying if Clint was home he would be the better parent.

When he asked if she was going to allow access, she tried to tell him she was worried about her children's welfare. He butted in and said, "Answer the question?" He told her that a lot when she tried to say something.

"I guess I'll have to," she finally said. "I don't want my children taken from me and I don't want to go to jail. I'll lose my income to support them." She knew there were guards outside the door by the elevator waiting to take her into custody.

She never had a chance. Who did she think she was, trying to take away the rights of grandparents?

In the end, the judge said, "This court is making an order in the best interest of the children." He's the court, for sure he is and he's looking out for us and the boys. Bless his heart or his gut. He gave us exactly what we asked for. If we'd wanted to, I think we could have the children half-time, Clint's half.

The judge gave Katie custody, saying, "It's too bad the other party is not here – is away." The other party, he called Clint. He wasn't much of a party most of the time.

The judge told Katie that she does not own those children and that she has to consider their needs, instead of trying to get one up on the grandparents. He said that if she didn't follow the court order she would find herself back in his court.

Wait now – here it is: the judge's exact words (I wrote them down). "There has been a significant injustice to these grandparents. I don't want to come back here, and have to face a situation where this order has not been followed because at that stage, then I'm going to have to do something that, perhaps, will hurt the children, and I don't want to do that, in fact, I don't know if I would ever do that. I could order that the police actually come and pick up the children. Do I want to do that? Absolutely not. I tell you, if that's what it takes to make you understand that you have to comply with the order, that's what I'll do. That's what I'll consider doing. I won't want to do it."

He didn't even try to corner Clint with a child support order. Between you and me, if I was the mother I'd want the judge held in contempt. I hope other grandparents happen on this judge – or, maybe he gave us some slack because he knows us. I'm glad that's over.

Guess what! She'll never find out that I had passports made up for the boys. Don't ask me how I managed that. You'd be surprised what you can get away with if you've got the mind for it. You know I do. Clint can take the boys out of the country to Mexico, leave them there if he wants to, and she'll never see them again. Serves her right.

Well, I must be off. I have to watch the televised church service now, maid. I got to get a pen. I see it on the screen, the number to call if you want a relationship with Jesus. It's a 1-800 number. For a love offering, they'll even send the book: *Jesus Saves; Why burn*? I'll get one for Katie so she can raise the boys right and keep them out of Hell. If she doesn't smarten up and follow Jesus that's where she's going.

I forgive you for your remarks about my son, because I sure as heck don't want unforgiveness to send me to Hell.

Love,

Velma, your sis, the one with the big heart

~ *Julia LeClair*

An expression from England about a politician or a dishonest business person: "He's so crooked his picture won't hang straight on the wall."

Woman on The Street

So, tell me, Old Hag,
What are you doing with a half-smoked
Cigar hanging off your drooping lips
As you suck back the brown spit,
drools hanging from your chin?

Don't tell me that thread-bare
Tweed coat still keeps you warm
in winter.
The bite of the wind must numb
Those gnarled fingers sticking out of
The holey snow-balled mitts you wear.

Why don't you go inside
Before the droppings on your nose
Freeze in icicles?

Say what?
You have no home
But this is Canada.
Surely God there must be somewhere
You can crawl in
Where hot soup warms you.
No?
Well, come to my house
For a cup of herb-laced tea
Guaranteed to put you
Out of your misery.

~ Jean Legge Hiscock

The Big "C"

Another excerpt from the Deer Pond Saga Interviews with Andrea Lee

(I fills in at darts Monday nights when Josie has Council meetings so I got to know Carlee and I was some sorry when she got the bad news. She's tough as nails in more ways than one. She's got a good heart and she's been through a lot, so never mind her rough edges. I thinks the world of her. Here's her story exactly the way she told it to me.)

I'm not the kind of person you'd expect to have a miracle. I knows that. I enjoys a beer on the weekends, sometimes a toke even after my shift at the bar. I loves dancing. As long as the music plays, I stays on the floor. Yes, I loves dancing. That's why the pain in my left leg right below my knee bothered me so much. I had to stop dancing. I was feeling achy and feverish, too. Thought I had the flu. Never came in my mind it might be the Big C.

When I got the diagnosis, I figured that was it. No miracles for me. I don't go to church much. I walks along the beach on Sunday morning, breathing in the fresh air, listening to the Powerhouse roar and the waves splish-splashing their smiles against the sand.

I met an old man more wrinkled than Saturday's paper crumbled up to go into the woodstove one morning. He said, "Nice to meet another convert to the Blue Sky Cathedral."

I knew what he meant. I feels closer to God on the beach than I ever do in church.

Anyway, you knows how it goes with the Big C. It's all about the D's: Doctors, diagnosis, denial, and desperation and finally – delivery or defeat.

I soon headed down the Defeat highway. The doctors said my chances to live much longer were slim to none with not too much space in between.

I don't have a family. I grew up in the System and never got attached to any of my paid "moms." They never got attached to me either. I gave them such a hard time, they used to check to see if my horns and tail had popped out.

I do have good friends and I get hugs – and shoulders to cry on. My friends don't treat me like the Big C is catching. Thank God.

The doctors said my days were numbered. I don't want to think about all the stuff before that: the biopsy, surgery, chemo, radiation while the Big C bulldozed over me.

One Sunday morning when the grass was still weeping its dewy tears and when all the world smelled fresh and new, the sky so blue it hurt, I went to my Cathedral and sat on a long, white dead tree, its roots sprawled apart like a woman with her skirt blown up in the wind. I slid down to the sand, leaned against the tree and thought about all my life, the good and the bad. Since I growed up. life was okay.

"God," I said, "I want to dance again. My leg hurts so much it's hard to walk even. Won't get to the beach much longer." I took deep breaths and thanked God I was here this minute, anyway. When I died, I hoped I'd go someplace as nice as this. I never ever hurt no one on purpose. I helps out when I can, does the best I can.

Swallows soared through the blue, telling me salmon was on their way. I fly fish. Maybe not this year.

I started to cry – cried till my tears washed away my regrets, cried until I was ever so tired.

"Okay God." I said, "You knows best. Please don't make me hurt too much before I dies."

The sun slipped in behind a cloud and I saw rays come down to the hills drawing up water. I wondered how it might feel to be drawn up to the heavens or to float down to the water and if I'd ever get to the beach again.

I shivered and watched the clouds move away and the sun come out, warming my face and my bare hands. A strange thing happened. A feeling I'd never had filled me, a heat, an energy throbbing through me, hitting most in spots where they'd told me the tumors were growing. I was scared I'd die right on the beach, scared, but okay, if it happened. What a good place to die!

A peace filled me, a knowing right to my centre, right in my bones. I knew I was getting better.

I rested until my strength came back. Then I walked to my old Honda Civic, drove home, and slept till next morning.

When I saw my doctor, he couldn't figure out how I got well. I knows. Honest to God, a miracle happened. Happened to me. Don't know why − or why I lost my best friend to the Big C. I'm nobody special. Maybe I have something to do while I keep on living. I'm getting my high school diploma through the GED program. Afterwards, I'll think on what to do next. Life sure tastes sweet.

~ Deborah Hedd

OUCH!

© Samantha A. Parsons

My Ouch Story
Grade One Assignment

OUCH! Last year I was at my friend's house. I hit my head off the TV stand. I yelled out and Carter C's parents came down. His dad carried me into the bathroom. Then he called my mom and dad. When they came, I got into the car and then I went to the hospital.

I waited and waited. I went inside the room and the person that was in there ripped the bandage off. When the person was done, I went to the doctor and had to lie down on the bed. When he put the stitches in my head, it really hurt, but I stayed as calm as I could. It was 5 stitches that the doctor put in my head. I didn't cry at the first part, but when the doctor was almost done, I started crying and he said, "It is okay. I am almost done."

And in a flash he was done and then I jumped in the car and got some ice cream and we drove home and when I got home my mom let me watch TV and that is the end.

~ *Aaron Kawaja*

Art is Neither Good or Bad.

It is Art.

MY DREAM HOUSE

My dream house would have a killion billion servants. It would have one humongous garden with tons of flowers. It would have a giant hot tub. It would be hot pink and blue. In my storage room there would be 10 hot pink and blue limos, and one killion jillion billion dollars protected by a one killion billion dollars security system. It would be as large as Buckingham Palace and another palace, combined together. The house would be on top of the Hollywood sign. I would get Nick Carter's family to build it so they would die faster. Everyday I would go to the machine room and get a machete. I would hire someone to decorate the Hollywood sign with flowers from my garden.

By: Carolyn

Inside of it is a hot tub, an indoor swimming pool. A theatre, a built-in go cart track, it so big it takes up five baseball fields. A motor bike race track, a rifle range. The house is all red and green, with an aquarium, 88 butlers, a built-in bar. Monster truck rally, sea-doo track, airport. A Ferrari. A big satellite dish, Hollywood.

By: Christopher

My dream house would be 7 stories high. With 18 bedrooms that have yellow walls, very smooth and king size beds in each one. A living room with a tv that has 49 channels. Painted blue with a green ceiling. 2 sofas and 3 love seats. Every cd in the world. 15 staircases. Red carpet in every room. A rec room with 7 tv's. 8 bathrooms with a hot tub, two sinks, and one toilet. A kitchen with everything I needed. It would be filled with servants. They will take care of everything I need done.

By: Erin

My dream house has chicks like Pamela Anderson and Sony and has 8,000 rooms. One is a go cart room, shooting room for my bad girls (dummies) built in bar and a swimming pool with a beach and it is the size of the ocean.

By: Gerry

My dream house would be really big. It would have a swimming pool, elevator, skating rink, and a mall in it. It would be black on the outside and yellow walls. It would be made out of wood. It would be built in California. It would have a five-floor patio. I would have a servant to do everything for me

By: Jena

I would like to live in the Princess Toadstool's castle. It is a huge castle in Nintendo 64 in a game: Super Mario 64. And I will get a million thousand 2200 and 63 hot tubs and 6 trillion pools. There will be a giant huge room filled with gold bricks. My house will be where my house is right now. I won't have to go to school. I will have a room covered with diamonds. My garden will be exactly like Princess Toadstool's garden.

By: Jennifer

Once I lived in a mansion. I asked my butler to do everything for me. I asked him to do so much stuff for me that he kicked me out. I lived on the street. I would live in a box; I would be so poor I could not paint the box.

By: Jessica

I would like a house that is wide and long with lots of rooms. I'd like to have the rooms that are so high up that you would have to use an elevator to get up there. In my house, I'd have six washrooms down stairs. I'd like one big hot tub in one room and I would have a jacuzzi in the rest of the washrooms. Oh yeah, I'd have sinks too. I'd have a big swimming pool in my BIG yard. My house would be made of gold. I'd have lots of dogs and horses. The horses would live in a farm.

By: Krystle-Lee

Has a hot tub, rifle range, built in tv, race car track, 8 butlers, built in bar, monster truck alley, sea-doo, S.S. Mustang and the inter-galactic satellite, and I'd live in Jamaica.

By: Matthew

I will have a 10-storey house. There will be a burger king. I will have a ski resort, my own teacher, my own roller coaster, a lot of cool rides, a pool with a high diver and water slide. I would live in Florida and have10 ski doos.

By: Megan

I would like to live in a mansion with warm water and a big swimming pool with warm water and I want a big bed just for me. I want a maid that does whatever I want. I want my mansion made of bricks of gold. Big shiny blocks of gold. I want my yard, the biggest in the world. I want a huge kitchen with two fridges, one with good food, the other with junk. My garden has a million flowers and a hammock.

By: Melanie

My dream house is under ground. I would like to have Shon Clod Van Dame. Under a tree in Africa to keep the rain away.

By: Scott

My dream house is the Buckingham Palace because Princess Diana walked on the floor. I would build it over the Hollywood Sign.

By: Unknown

Let Me Sing to You Anyhow

© Victoria Young Kawaja

The Wait

What do I do
while I wait
For this grandchild?
S/he is still a tiny being,
heart beating gently:
diminutive body
curved towards itself,
tiny hands curled
inside my child.

Child of my child,
s/he is of me,
cradled by God:
Kayleigh or Nicholas
Waiting to see.

~ *Nellie P. Strowbridge*

Surrogate Creator

In the circle of my womb,
in its darkness you came into being,
the beat of your heart God's,
his breath yours.

I am God's surrogate,
my belly shaped into
an alabaster globe,
broken to let you out, my firstborn,
born in
a baptism of blood and water.

~ *Nellie P. Strowbridge*

Dream of the dead, expect to hear of a baby's birth.

Small One

I sat dumbstruck when you were born,
Tears of joy quietly seeping down my cheek.

I could see the future, and what I saw
Was a large part of the world
Held in your tiny hands.

It left me in awe, with a sense of calmness,
an internal swelling in feelings of pride.
I thought of all the tears of happiness
You would bring me in our years together.

You reached me in a way
I never thought anyone could, small one.
Your little fingers reached into my future,
Touched it in places I didn't know were there.

Sweet thing, I know my voice is not famous.
Won't you let me sing to you anyhow?
Be kind enough to smile now and then,
When I do, if I please you.

My song may be a small one,
But every note is filled with the warm,
Deep love and satisfaction,
You've created inside of me.

That, little one, is not small in the least.

~ Jamie Stuckless

Kristen

Her chubby cheeks
Cheerfully glow.
She's laughing
At what, she doesn't know.

She shakes her rattle
And sucks her thumb.
Who would have known
Something so simple could be so fun?

Then she cries
And you wonder what is wrong.
She seemed cheerful before,
happy all along.

Does she need her diaper changed?
Who knows what to do?
Maybe she's hungry;
She could be teething, too.

Hush little baby;
Cry no more.
Mommy will soon be here
And I'll be out the door!

~ Stacey Hiscock-Pittman

Written at a student workshop many years ago.

Momma

Please don't cry for me, Momma....you don't see me, but I am still here.
I flew to heaven gently, Momma....it was painless and without fear.

Please don't cry for me, Momma....you don't see me, but I am still here.
If you miss my sweet scent, Momma....hold my teddy tight and near.

Please don't cry for me, Momma....you don't see me, but I am still here.
Look around you, Momma....in my fingerprints you'll find me there.

Please don't cry for me, Momma....you don't see me, but I am still here.
When you are sound asleep, Momma....in your dreams I will appear.

Dedicated to Ashley, Autumn and Freya's mother

~ Kayla Critch

My Dad Was a Miner

My dad was a miner
He worked under the ground we walked on
And while we skipped along the grass
And the fields of yellow flowers
He pushed through the ore mines
Covered in red dust and muck

We were always so excited for his return
Everyday we waited for his step
And I know our mother dreaded
The sound of that siren when it screamed
echoing the sound of her own fear
of a day when he would not come home

He came home every day
And the mines died before he did
His new job pulled him far away
From the danger of the dripping and savaged rock
To places of light and beautiful country
Till death found him and claimed him after all

I remember his smile always
His eyes danced and his heart was kind
He sang to his little ones
Bounced them on his knee and teased them
With wrestling matches and pony rides
He made music with bottles, water and string

All these years later I think of him,
The pride he would have felt for his children
Knowing how far each has gone,
proud and successful every one

He left us much too early
His children, his wife

~ Cynthia Babb Fry

I Remember Her Still

I remember her still
As she dashed about
Skipping her rope
With a song and a shout

Time! It has passed
The years they have flown
My baby too quickly
Into a woman has grown

The day she left home
Past a tear in my eye
To live her own life
She was going to try

Her mind it was filled
With doubts and with fears
I knew she would make it
Despite her young years

~ Ray Bennett

When a baby stares at the ceiling or at a corner of the room, he is watching angels. No wonder he smiles!

A Salted Soul?

The unique inner voice
Haunts endlessly
She was born with
Crystals of salt
Embedded deeply in her bones

The flow of life
Brought maturity - only in years -
She sits endlessly
Watching the sea gulls
Screech and dive
Entranced by the sound
Of waves gently kissing
The beach

Forever she shall be
A child in a world of her own
Drenched to the bone
By the whispering wind
And memories
Too wild and far too
Transient
To pen

~ *Minnie J. Vallis*
(1933 - 2013)

Spring Pleasures

Ragamuffin, barefoot boy
Little face alight with joy,
Alder slung across his back
Luncheon in a paper sack.

Off he goes at break of day
Whistling cheerfully on the way.
Without a worry, thought or care,
His to enjoy – this clean, fresh air.

At the deepest pools he'll lie in wait
And watch the trout rise for his bait,
Till very soon the morn is spent.
He'll lie back and snooze in deep content.
For fame and fortune he has no wish;
He longs to enjoy those luscious fish.
Then homeward he winds his way,
Content to have lived another day.

There he meets at the turn of the road,
An ardent angler with precious load,
An expensive rod, and reel and kit,
For which the fish care not a bit.
He'll do his best till the set of sun,
To try and catch the wary one,
Then home he'll plod at the end of day
And tell of the ones that got away.

~ *Nico LaBlanc*
(Blanc Penney)
(1927 - 1989)

A New Beginning

When I was crying
You wiped away my tears.
When I was afraid
You soothed my fears.

When I needed a friend
You were there.
When I felt lonely
You held me near.

When I did wrong
You loved me still.
You took care of me
When I was ill.

You took me in
When I was left alone.
You loved me
Like I was your own.

I was lost
You found me.
I was blind
You helped me see.

We've had some bad times,
Good times too.
What would I do
Without both of you?

Now that I realize
What you did,
I'm grateful and glad
I'm your foster kid.

~ *Natasha Strickland*

Dedicated to my Aunt and Uncle

Not Kissing Cousins

I don't know where to start. Mom always says, "Start at the beginning."

Here goes. In the beginning…. That sounds like the Bible and believe me this story is not like the Bible. Okay, maybe it is. I mean, how else did the human race ever start? Who did the kids of Adam and Eve marry if they didn't keep it in the family? A monkey? The serpent? An alien?

Yeah. This story is Bible-like. Okay, I am talking brothers and sisters getting together. Not cousins. I don't think they're cousins. The closest they are is what Mom calls "fark cousins". You know what that is: two cousins related somewhere along the family tree far enough down the line so that if they have a baby, it will not be a little monster. I don't think we're even talking about fark cousins, in the born-in-the-family kind of way.

You tell me though, do you think it's right for two people who slept in the same crib, sucked from the same breast, and ate at the same table for years, do you think it's right for those two to kiss?

Sally Ann and Joe Jack are closer than two Velcro-stuck tabs. I think it's sick. Sally Ann got took in with us when her mother died two days after she was born. Since my Mom was nursing Jack, she nursed Sally Ann, too.

Mom said she'd look after Sally Ann until someone came to get her; no one ever came so she kept Sally Ann forever. Never signed any papers and no one asked her to.

Sally Ann is prettier than the first crocus that pokes up in spring when snow is still pushing at the wall of the house except where the heat leaks out. Joe Jack is cuter than a ground hog announcing winter is over. So you can see why they were drawn to each other.

I don't think they got a right to go and kiss, though. Sally Ann will not kiss me. I'm not as cute as either one of them. At least I am not related in the way they are. I mean, I lives with them but Mom never nursed me. Her breasts went dry as soon as I was born. I'm the oldest so she always says she's happy she did better second and third and fourth time around. I never gets the best of anything!

100

I saw Sally Ann and Joe Jack kissing out behind the barn. Twice. I knows they're only five. I'm seven, old enough to be responsible for my sins, Mom says.

And I knows that kissing someone who nursed with you is wrong. I don't care what anyone says, it's a real bad start.

~ *Deborah Hedd*

The two friends were the last ones called in for interviews. They did want the jobs but they had always had problems in school with English, spelling and vocabulary. After the interviews they agreed they'd done well after all.

Bailey: *They asked me to use some words in a sentence:*
Dana: *What words?*
Bailey: *They talked funny for educated people. Wanted me to make a sentence using "defence" and "defeat."*
Dana: *What did you say?*
Bailey: *Oh, that was easy. I said, 'When de horse jumped over de fence, de feet went over before de head.'*
Dana: *That was a good answer. They asked me to use "fascinate" in a sentence. I had to think, but I came up with a good answer.*
Bailey: *What did you say?*
Dana: *'I had a yellow jacket, it had nine buttons but I could only fasten eight.'*

A Pastel Hymn

I was a pilgrim
Upon an innocent stream
With the rim of my mouth
Half-submerged
In the skim of a milky ribbon
Gliding through the naked ripples
Of her shoulder

She fed me
From dimples and palms
The plush petals of lilies
And the echoes of my heart flowed into her nape
Sleeping in her silky song

Then I filled
My breath with reverence
And sank into the gleaming of her eyes
Where forsaken goddesses and runaway boys
Surge in the place of completeness.

~ *Matthew Spence*

Between You and Me

I love you so much.
I guess that's why sometimes I get impatient
waiting
Wondering when we'll finally be
Together all the time.
I know it has to be this way for now.
doing the right thing.
I trust our love is strong enough, that
Someday soon we'll
Walk, and talk, touch and love each other the way
We've wanted to.

It's difficult sometimes
I want you so much now.
Our time will come, and
when it does, it will be right −

And very, very beautiful.

~ *Terry Manuel*
(1961 – 2017

"You can't tell the mind of a squid."
     A squid moves backwards and forwards. An untrustworthy person's
actions are unpredictable.

Album of Love

There are gems in this world worth millions
Their beauty could never compare
With the picture of love in my album
Of the lady with the soft, golden hair.

In my Album of Love is your picture
So deeply engraved from the start.
In my Album of Love is your picture
And the Album of Love is my heart.

All the clouds in my life turned to sunshine
And these dark nights are only a dream,
As I awake to remember your picture,
You're my goddess of love and my queen.

My heart is on fire and burning
As I gaze on the face that I love,
The face of the one in the picture
That's engraved in my Album of Love.

~ Arthur Ball
(1912 – 1998)

Love Is Love

Love can begin
At the very first glance
In a moment in time
When she first grabs your hand.

Love may begin
When it's not on your mind
And the last thing you thought
Was love that you'd find.

No matter the moment
Place or the time
A man or a woman
You don't have to hide.
For love is beautiful
It shouldn't be kept inside.

Be true to yourself
Don't live in a lie
Walk proudly beside her
Holding onto her hand
Show the world it's okay
That you're not with a man.

There will be haters
Those who don't understand
Trying to change you
hold your fate in their hands.

Follow your heart
Show them it can be
That two women together
Can create a family.

For God makes no mistakes
He is never wrong
Be proud of yourself
Wherever your heart may belong.

~ *Deanna Mcdeiros*

Desire

When you and I are apart.
Can sorrow break my Lonely Heart.
I Love You. Honest I Do.
Sleep is sweet when I dream of you.
All the world is like a Rose.
Night is Near so I must close.
With care, read the first word in every line.
You will find what's on my mind.

~ Terry Manuel
(1961 – 2017)

Chris and Sandy were having a great time when Chris glanced out the window and saw Sandy's spouse pulling into the driveway.

Chris opened the window. "Quick! Jump, Sandy, jump before Charlie gets in."

"But, Sandy, we're thirteen floors up!"

"JUMP, Chris! This is no time to be superstitious."

Love Your Mom & Dad

I often sit and wonder why young people are so
Troubled today.
Is it the world in which we live,
Or the strange things we hear them say?

If only youth would sit for just a while,
Talk to their Mom and Dad
Many problems could be solved.
Their sweet smiles would make them glad.

Some say Mom and Dad don't really care
about what they are going through.
If only they would look deep in their hearts,
They would know, that it's not true.

Many sleepless nights they spent with you
From the time you were a babe.
Now it's time to realize this gift,
The love and life your parents gave.

When you are lonely and down-hearted,
Turn to Mom and Dad with care.
You will never know what love is,
Until God takes them to his home, up there.

~ Daphne Russell

My Mother

My mother always coaxed me to write
I said I would, maybe, I might

Now my mother's gone
Only her memories live on

A quiet woman, she had strong ways
It was needed in those early days
She washed by hand and chopped her own wood
The children helped her as little children could
She brought water from the brook
Despite the many hours this chore took
She didn't complain; that wasn't her way
She did all she could to her dying day

My mother always coaxed me to write
I said I would, maybe, I might

~ Florence Antle

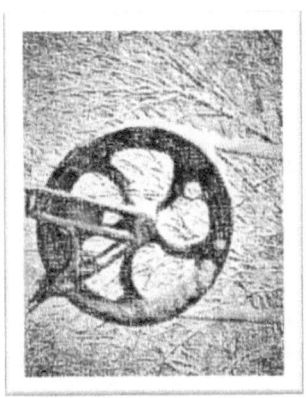

A Vision of an Independent Writer

The river flowed both ways. The current moved from north to south. It still fascinated Bianca even after all the years of watching. The dawn had lifted the morning air and it was filled with swallows. Their wings brushed the water. Her daughter, Kaitlyn, had gone away; she must have left early in the morning. She noticed a sheet of a paper inserted in the typewriter on the kitchen table, her work place for writing. Kaitlyn knew her mother would be certain to find it there.

Please do not get all uptight, Mom I can look after myself. I'm going out west alone at least for now - if Andy phones, tell him I need some time alone to think.

Kaitlyn was just eighteen, not dry behind her ears. Bianca had never liked Dean. And now he's driven her away. Bianca prays to God things will work out for her. She thinks, I have too much work on my hands to fret over Kaitlyn. Lucky me, I've got my work to take my mind off my problems. At forty-nine, that's not such a terrible state of affairs. If I hadn't been a writer, I might have been a mess at this point and time of my life.

Bianca read Kaitlyn's letter again, made coffee and sat looking at the birds in the bird house outside her window; she glanced at the river again. Matthew, her husband, was away for a few days fishing off-shore. He loved the water, it was part of him since childhood. The house seemed too quiet as she looked around and saw the pictures of her children. All but Kaitlyn have already grown up and gone away.

She wandered around the house. In the basement she found some old snap shots in Ma's old cabinet.

A man with a woman and child were standing by a gate. The man, tall and strong-looking, had dark skin, and the woman was small with light brown, short hair. Bianca recognized several trees in the background: spruce, fir, pear, blueberry, raspberry, and more. We had a beautiful garden, she remembers.

In the photograph, she is the child, about two years old, with curly blonde hair. Her small dog, Tip, looks up at her. He always followed Bianca around the yard, keeping an eye on her. Bianca's mother allowed Tip to sleep in Bianca's bedroom to keep her company. Her father always had time for her; he lifted her on top of the gate, holding her so she wouldn't fall. He was a farmer and always smelled of the fresh air.

She recalls, I lived in that house around the time Ma and Dad took sick. I had to be very quiet. Mrs. Elizabeth, our neighbour with grey hair, always worn in a bun style, came and did the cooking and caring for me. I often wanted to see my parents but wasn't allowed because of the "virus". I felt very lonely and afraid.

Then one evening the doctor came and spoke to Mrs. Elizabeth outside alone on the bridge.

When she went back into the house, she spoke to Bianca, "You are a strong little girl, your parents are going to a better place."

Bianca cried and was hurt. "What better place than to be here with Bianca! Why did God do this?" The next day, she went and visited the room in their house and everything had vanished.

Mrs. Elizabeth said, "My child, you are going to be living with Mr. and Mrs. Banks; He worked with your Dad years ago, and they offered to take you. They have no children of their own; they are kind."

Bianca said nothing; she has learned you can't argue when you are a child. As they drove off with Mrs. Elizabeth, Bianca looked back, watching the farm gate closing.

She recalls that the land, furniture and house was sold to pay the mortgage, but she also found out years later, Mrs. Elizabeth managed to smuggle the piano and a few other things from the house. The old trunk and the cabinet ended up with the Banks.

When she arrived at the Banks, they were waiting. They lived in a huge brick house on top of the hill, Mr. Banks was a big man and Mrs. Banks was a small woman. They hugged Bianca and told her. "You can stay as long as you want.

In the morning, Mrs. Banks took her to school. At first, Bianca hated it. There were different classes of kids. She met her teacher, Mrs. Noseworthy a tiny woman with black hair; she was waving her hand for everyone to listen. She always had a special care for Bianca's needs. After school, they often walked around the park near the school, to look for bird nests and to watch the swans in the brook.... Memories of the past....

Bianca goes to bed late. At six-thirty AM the telephone rings, she has never been an early or easy awakener. Who would be calling this early?

Kaitlyn, of course! "Mother I want to come home. Is that okay?"

She wants to come home! She's come to her senses.

"Yes, Kaitlyn, come home

Bianca arranged Kaitlyn's flight home. She will deal with Kaitlyn when she gets here. She learned how to cope day by day when she lost her parents. One day at a time.

The telephone rang again. A stranger's voice said, "Mrs. Stevens you don't remember me, but I was in the Coles Bookshop last September, when you were doing a book-signing "*Spare the Innocence*." Well, Mrs. Stevens I do a lot of writing myself, and I'd be grateful if you would explain to me how you got started. Well I mean did you know some person in the publishing field?"

"I don't know," Bianca said, I kept sending stories out; I wrote a novel and a publisher was interested in it. I worked a lot of long hours, it's awfully early. I really can't help you." She slammed the telephone down.

Bianca picks up the receiver. Was she too rude? The woman only wanted advice. Bianca was worrying about Kaitlyn. One day at a time, that philosophy didn't always work.

Michael, a neighbour, came to the door.

"Hi, come in, would you like some tea? Matthew's out fishing." She tells Michael about Kaitlyn; "You worry too damn much about her! You were married at her age."

When Michael left, she looked at the snapshots again. She remembered coming home; everything was always neat and the smell of homemade bread and cookies, drifted out to meet her and her friend, Kay. They met in elementary school. They were friends until they finished school.

Often Bianca went outside to a play house. She remembers a cellar where she hoped to find treasures and did find some jewelry. She did not think it was of any value and gave it to neighbours.

She opens the old cobwebbed trunk from the cellar. She finds a snapshot. In the photograph, she is nine years old with friends of her Ma. She finds dishes painted purple that belonged to her grandmother.

Memories flooded over her. Bianca was not afraid of anything in the Banks' house. She always felt safe in her room at night with; peach ruffled curtains and lovely quilts. She loved the hooked mat on her floor. She was happy to have a chamber pot for her own use, especially on cold winter nights. She recalls old songs her Ma sung to her before she died and how they reminded her of her mother when Mrs. Banks sang the words to her. She closed the trunk and touched her old sewing machine. Mrs. Banks sewed for her and the neighbours. She keeps the sewing machine because of the memories it holds. If it could talk, what stories it could tell.

Bianca waits for Kaitlyn with hope, with fear. She wants to write but the words will not come. Her stories while she waits are as silent as those told by the photographs, the dishes, the trunk. She sighs and goes to the typewriter on her desk. She'll begin with the story of how she came to be a writer. She'll worry about Kaitlyn when she walks through the door.

~ *Anne Bowring*

Twice Loved

I could easily see how happy they were
as they strolled hand in hand.
It wouldn't be long, I felt at the time,
till they shared a wedding band.

It was that big quarrel they had, I suppose,
that drove him off to war.
Soon after that, we heard he had died.
Love had abandoned her, for sure.

When she came to me for comfort one day,
I, his best friend, was near
to dry her tears and hold her close,
and I began to really care.

We missed him so much, the both of us,
though his life was over and done.
The living cannot stay in the past,
so a bright, new love had begun.

I made her happy as she made me
as wonderful times went by,
Then one day a letter came
and she began to cry.

He hadn't died, the message said.
He was a prisoner for over a year.
Now he was coming to claim his love.
I understood her tears.

Tormenting feelings possessed her mind
each day and each night, too.
Most women had one man to love.
My wife, she had two.

We're expecting him at our door any time.
Then we'll tell him our point of view,
how our fondness for him brought us together
and stirrings within us grew.

Perhaps they'll stroll holding hands once more
as they did in times past long ago.
'Twould please my heart to have them do that.
Still, she'll return to me, I know.

I feel assured what we share is real,
their love a youth's memory.
He may have stolen her heart back then,
Her future is with me!

~ *Karen Bennett*

Do not light three cigarettes with the same match. This will surely bring bad luck to the third person.

A Trapper's Wife

They say it's not a woman's life
To be a trapper's wife
Long days, cold nights
The blizzard strikes like a blinding light.

Days she doesn't help at the traps
She grooms the furs
Of wolf, fox, beaver and muskrat
With skillful hands she strips away
The layers that do not need to stay
Molded with a steady hand
A garment of softness and warmth
Unlike any in the land.

She cleans the meat and cures it all
Provisions for the coming fall
She sees to the children throughout the day
And not a word will you hear her say
You chop the wood
She prepares the meal
Tonight, you'll have rabbit, caribou or seal.

Now night returns in an already darkened land
On a stool by the stove she holds the fur in her hand
And as the night slowly slips away
She prepares for the very next day,

For in her heart she loves this life
And proudly proclaims
She's a trapper's wife.

~ *George T. Tucker*

The Gun and the Door

Since it happened, I sometimes stare at the golden shadows in the door as if I'm in a trance. That door has been there since I was a child, its crystal knob akin to the magnified solitaire diamond I hoped to get in a gold ring when I met the man of my daydreams.

The light, coming through the porch window, shines on the door when someone opens it, making tall, dark shadows. I always look at the shadows instead of the door. I've done that with doors as long as I can remember. When it is night and there is no light from the window on the door, the shadow is smaller, the reflection of a face clearer.

As if doors were for anything other than keeping some people out and other people in, some visitors have come in through the door and reached their hands up to grab the top of it to stretch tight muscles. I've wished I could reach so far.

Still, I sense a sinister presence to doors. When I was ten, my younger brother Sid lost a fingertip in the sharp bite of a slammed door. I stood shocked at the sight of blood from the severed finger dripping down its spine in coloured tears. It startled me more than Sid's cry for me to get his fingertip. I found it lying on the floor like a bloodied white grub. The doctor sewed the tip back on Sid's finger and now he has only a white scar to show that one part of his finger was ever parted from the other.

I face that porch door every day. I never know what's behind it. When a knuckle knocks against it or when someone pushes it open without knocking, it yawns open; its tight hinges squeak. Now the crystal knob is gone, leaving an empty round ring. On bright days, the sun shines through the front porch window and sunshine slants on the floor like the hall light does when my bedroom door is opened at night.

Sid left home when he got married and, after Daddy died, I married Bill who lived next door. He gave me a plain gold band; then he moved in with me.

One day, Bill flung back his head and let out a gush of laughter at something silly he'd said. His head danced back and forth. Then it jerked and hit the edge of the porch door. The door held steady and Bill's skull took the full impact.

I could see by the way Bill's eyes fluttered and he crumpled to the floor that he was injured. I am in a wheelchair so I couldn't go to him. It is only my voice that is strong, shrill sometimes because of my frustrations. I have to call for help quite often. Bill always fetched things for me: my cigarettes, my books and – well never mind – the list varies from day to day. Bill knew when he married me, the burden I would be on him. He said that love is an air cushion.

I called Bill's name until he stirred to consciousness and stood up. He bent down for me to feel where he had hit the door. I saw a soft rise similar to a large sebaceous cyst on the top of his head. His dark hair covered it so I couldn't see if bruised blood covered the lump.

Bill seemed fine for a while. Sometimes, though, he would stare at me and one day he grabbed a mystery novel I was reading. I had seven pages left to finish and I was anxious to find out if the villain got killed. Bill tore out the last few pages; a fistful of paper crumbled in his hand. Then he laughed.

I looked at him, and I wondered about him. Not for too long. I let myself forget about what he had done. It was only sometimes that he wasn't himself.

One time, his eyes went strange as if he didn't see me. Other people noticed changes in him; then they seemed to get used to the new Bill. He slapped me once. I cried; he laughed. Then it was as if he forgot what he'd done. Sometimes he'd lie in bed whimpering that he had a headache much like a child would complain about a toothache.

Then one day, Bill lifted my father's breech loader off the rack on the wall and pointed it at me. After all I'd been through with that gun – he knew it too. I felt my own eyes take on a strange look. Here I was trapped in a chair looking into the barrel of a gun that I had faced years before when I was a child. It's the reason I'm in this wheelchair.

My father had come home from bird hunting and laid the gun in the corner of the porch behind the door. Sid picked it up. He must have pointed it at my back as I was going in the hall towards my bedroom. The finger that had been injured in the door was on the trigger and he couldn't have been able to feel anything or he would have known he was squeezing hard. I was only twelve. I remember the feel of something, as if a hammer hit my back. Then I felt as if my spine had shattered into shards of glass. In the shadow of my bedroom door I watched myself fall.

Now my eyes were on Bill and I was saying in a shaky voice, "Give me the gun."

His voice came back, high-pitched: "It's all over; life is all over."

The grandfather clock chimed twice and Bill repeated his words, "It's all over," and then, "life and time all over." His arm moved swiftly and the clock's glass cover splintered. Shards fell to the floor; fragments hit my face. I noticed that the hands had fallen as if they were loose arms, the face fell off the clock. Bill was reloading the gun.

"Give me the gun." My voice faltered, then steadied itself. I felt as cold as steel as I added, "or you'll be sorry."

Suddenly Bill, his face in a fixed expression, leaned toward me. I reached for the gun. It slipped from his hands to mine. I held—for the first time, the thing that had maimed me. At first, I pointed it at the door. Then I pointed it at Bill. I didn't mean to pull the trigger. I don't know why I did. I wanted to get rid of the gun. I wanted to blow it apart. I screamed as pieces of Bill's head filled the air like a burst red balloon and splattered the walls and the porch door. He fell like a sack of flour; I threw the gun down where he lay.

The police didn't suspect me. They were told of Bill's strange ways. The gun was wiped and put back on the rack.

At the funeral, I turned to see Bill's brother, Luke, coming into the church. For a moment I thought it was Bill; I wanted to go to him. I felt myself running into his arms. I would have thought I was imagining it; other people saw it, too, and wondered what kind of power there is in grief. Luke laid me back in my chair and I was wheeled home.

When the door opens now and someone comes in with my meals, I imagine that Bill is back. Sometimes I see blood dripping down the door or on the door facing, little red teardrops that fell from my brother's finger after I closed the door on it. I scream. No one asks me why. They think I've gone as mental as Bill was.

I could have shot the door instead of Bill. It wasn't the door's fault that Bill got in its way. It was Bill that changed, not the door. It opened and shut the same as always. Still, a door can reflect too much, becoming a distorted mirror with shadows of those who darken them. Sometimes I think I see Bill's face in it, shining through the dark veneer in the dents and scrapes he made with this fists and nails when he was angry.

Doors turn rooms into secret compartments in a house. So many things can happen behind a door. They carry voices in their hinges. I can hear my father's voice calling himself a *bitch* loader. I was lucky I didn't have to have a shotgun wedding; it wouldn't have been Bill's fault.

Still, I could have been put in jail with bars to look at − instead of doors. Since I'm here, I should paint all the doors in the house white, smudge away their shadows with a paint roller. I could get rid of all the doors. After all, I must not be distracted by a door. I have to keep my eye on that gun. If I put myself up a bit I can reach the rack and get it.

No one better treat me the way Bill did.

~ *Nellie P. Strowbridge*

Current Affair

His name was Current, First Initial A;
Her name was Millie Watt and they met one day.
It was during a party by a couple they knew;
They looked at each other and their fuses all blew.

Their eyes were stuck to each other all night.
They couldn't stay separate, try as they might.
Enwrapped in each other, time seemed to pass;
At the pure speed of light, night vanished so fast.

Next day they were at it all over again,
All over each other in spite of the rain;
And sparks were a'flying all over the place
From Current's fast heartbeat to Millie's young face.

Current said, "Preacher, marry us now!"
The preacher said, "Sorry, I don't know how.
You two aren't compatible because of your C
For you are an A and she is a D."

~ Fred Stewart
(1934 - 2007)

The Life of a Flower

Morning	Noon	Night
He entered the store	He turned the key	Her world became
Knowing what	Carried her	Dark and grey
He was looking for	Into his home	She bloomed no more
He walked slowly	He placed her on the	He no longer
Looking at	Pedestal	Spoke to her
All the blooms	In the window	She felt herself
Breath-taking	He spoke to her	Wither away
He thought	Often	One evening
He wanted	She loved to be	She heard
A young one	In the sun	The key turn
One he could	She grew	As he entered
Tweak	Bloomed	She heard him speak
Her colour	Beautifully	As he walked
Would have	He worked	To the window
To match his décor	Longer	She watched
Then he saw her	Got home	As he placed
Surrounded	Later	His new flower
By others	Forgot to	In her old spot
Still	Water her	He turned
She stood out	Her branches drooped	Picking her up
She radiated	Her blooms fell off	He opened
Joy, youth, strength	He moved her	The waste disposal
He picked her up	To a corner	Her silent scream
With a smile	Out of the light	Was not heard
Of triumph	She felt her roots	As she fell into
He purchased her	Dry up	The darkness below

~ Jackie Sheppard Alcock

Unbalanced

Meshed together
Disconcerted
Chaotic thoughts
Tangled pandemonium
Cobwebs or words
Muddled, confused
No switch to shut down
Wired like an explosive
Breaking point unknown
Continuous torture of imperfections
Invisible to the human eye
Flawless exterior
Brilliant tendencies
Inherited mutated genes
Cell circuit disoriented
Constant struggle for diversion
Defense barrier warped
Chemicals or seclusion
To halt the process
Of eruption

~ Daisy Bennett-Lush

Chaos

You say "sorry"
as you grab for your coat
I am faint of heart
Emotionally wrecked
Singing of old things
Talking to the dead
Inside the days and nights
I look, yet I cannot see
Fight, yet I am not free
After a lifetime of learning
I feel stupid
Confusion leads to clarity
Water overflows a bowl

Take the arrows away from Cupid
He is shooting at my soul
He comes back again and again
Steals my trust
Other unmentionable stuff

Judging each other never get us far
Changing the core of who you are is hard
When you do
Not long after, you will be missing you
We have been charting our progress on a graph
Losing our ability to laugh
Praying the scientist is right
Praying clarity comes from chaos tonight

~ Roxanne Abbott

What Is That Racket?

The house it did shiver;
The timbers did squeak.
The first time I heard it,
I was unable to speak.
I clung to the bed post
To stay off the floor,
And then I remembered
My wife she does snore.

What's that racket;
Oh what's that din?
Did it come from without,
Or did it come from within?
I dashed to the window;
I ran to the door,
And then I remembered:
My wife she does snore.

It's two in the morning;
The shades are all drawn.
I hear a great murmur
Out on the front lawn.
I peek out the window,
And lo and behold:
Our neighbours are standing
Out there in the cold.

I tell them quite calmly –
And this is a fact –
My furnace is old
And is starting to act.
It's okay by day,
But by night it does roar.
I just couldn't tell them,
My wife she does snore.

I return to the house
Somewhat relieved.
But I know that little
Has been achieved.
Now she is dreaming
Of some distant shore.
I know, I can tell
By the way she does snore.

~ *Ray Bennett*

ZZZ

ZZZZ

ZZZZ

Dump Kitty

Found on the classified, a kitten who was free.
A family thought I was cute, came and got me.
They brought me home to my bed.
"Love you forever," is what they said.
Months passed by, and I played alone.
Forgot the love that I was shown.

One day I was picked up, put in a crate,
Put in a car and dropped by a gate.
I walked through the rubble.
Where did they go?
Where was the food? I did not know.
Others like me had passed on by.
With patches of fur or missing an eye.
Why am I left here? What did I do?
They got a new kitty all tiny and new.

I made some friends; they keep me warm.
We snuggle together in rain and snowstorm.
The day may come when I might be found,
But trust is not easy, the second time 'round.

Dedicated to all the lost and forgotten

~ Kayla Critch

Wistful

Look at Sadie
Stretched out
On her favourite spot
On the back of her
Big fluffy chair

She stares out into the night
And I think
She is wistful
She is missing
Someone

I sit on the
Sofa opposite her
In our room
The dim light of
The lone lamp
While the soft
Snowflakes fall
Illuminated
By the patio lights

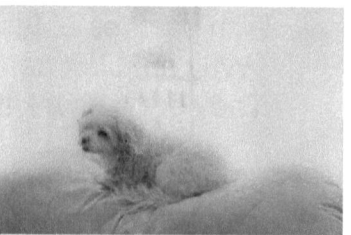

We share this wistfulness
Alone together

~ Cynthia Babb Fry

Mirrors and Boxes

Caroline says she's glad there are mirrors to show her looks, even though she doesn't like what she sees. She often wonders what it would be like to grow up and get old and suddenly see oneself in the mirror for the first time. Sometimes now, if she stands looking at her reflection long enough, it seems as if the mirrored face belongs to a stranger. She wonders what her face tells other people about her feelings. She smiles, resigned. Her hair, the colour of steel wool, is loosely curled all over her head. Her face is soft and full and her eyes are a sharp blue. Her chin is sagging and starting to form a line for another chin.

Carol, who still has only one chin and lots of short, dark hair, knows she'll have the face and body of her mother someday. Sometimes she feels her mother is inside her, affecting her movements and voice.

Caro-Lin, Carol's daughter, whose dark hair springs all over her head and down her back in gusts of curls, shows hints that she has the pleasantly defined face and eyes her mother and grandmother once had. Carol-Lin rolls her eyes when someone tells her that she resembles them.

Caroline tells her daughter about her dreams. "In one dream," she says, "I open a box to see what's inside, only to find another box, and inside it a smaller box." She sighs. "There is no end to boxes lining other boxes."

Carol knows that her mother is a larger box, she is a medium box, and Carol-Lin is a smaller box. Their names have a verbal linkage symbolizing that they are still a part of each other, though separate physically and in their values.

Carol's dreams are kept to herself. They go into an invisible compartment. Sometimes she loses her identity in the nether world of her dreams. "I never dream anything that can't happen – do I?" she asks herself. Her eyes meet their image in her bedroom mirror.

Brendan, Carol's husband, accuses her of falling asleep in the middle of her own sentences. He mumbles the word narcolepsy. She hears him, but she doesn't answer as her mind becomes the stuff her daymares are made of, mixing up pieces of her life in distorted images. *She's chasing a spider that has the face of Pussy Cat, a dog she owned when she was ten. The spider has bat wings and is flying through the air. It pitches on her bed. She lifts a hammer to kill it. Just as she lowers the hammer, it touches the crown of Brendan's shiny, bald head.*

Carol wakes up in the middle of Brendan's sentence. She notices how full his head of hair is, as if she is seeing it for the first time.

Caroline, Carol and Caro-Lin are in a white sports car driving along the highway. Caro-Lin, who has been a teenager for four years, is at the wheel. Up ahead is a large, red stop sign. Carol cries, "Stop!" Caro-Lin laughs. Then suddenly they are on top of a highway edged in red, the same colour as the sign. Carol-Lin can't stop. A substance comes out from Carol's body like a bubbly blanket. It grows and grows until it encloses her daughter. Carol's head feels as if it is going to explode as they go into the air and disappear into oblivion.

It's just one more dream about her daughter. She is no longer sure of her place in her daughter's life. Such a short time ago, she was a cute little rascal in the crib, drooling over her rail. Now she is drooling over some strange boy – back to keeping her mother awake at night. Carol mutters, "She has her days and nights mixed up, wanting to be up romping at night and asleep in the morning."

She stares in the mirror at her silver hairline. It's as if the tip of a wet paint brush has accidently touched her dark hair. Daughters on the loose, not ageing causes this, she thinks.

Behind her, Carol-Lin comes and tips her head over her mother's shoulder. Two sets of eyes stare into the mirror.

Carol is persuaded to let her daughter spend the weekend at her boyfriend's home. Up to this point she never knew what mothers went through when daughters got on the loose. These creatures they once gave their life's milk to at the risk of having their nipples bitten off.

The first time Carol takes Carol-Lin to Kirk's place, she wonders why she is doing it. Perhaps because the feel of spring is on her skin as fresh as a bath, and life is in the air, and though she feels it is her responsibility to dilute the temptations of sex for her daughter, she doesn't want to stunt the life that surges in her – her expectations to find love.

Carol leaves her daughter with a family she has never met before in a place she's never been before. She knows that she can't tell if people are nice after only a half hour of smiles and conciliatory chit chat. The teenagers, who have the devil-knows-what on their minds, grin bashfully while the adults talk.

After leaving Carol-Lin with strangers, to be there for two days, she misses her turnoff to the highway and ends up on top of a hill that she thought would lead her back home. Instead, she's on the edge of a cliff above the sea. She doesn't dare look up at a curtained window, aware that someone could be watching this crazy woman who loses her way on the community's only street.

Emotional pain is much stronger than physical pain, she thinks, as she drives home. She wishes Carol-Lin was on her breast right now. She wouldn't even care if it was at a time when she was teething and Carol's blood and milk mingled.

Carol doesn't want her daughter's body to be contaminated by a strange boy's gutter needs. She hears about other teenagers getting pregnant. Caroline thinks sex between young people without legal or moral sanction is dirty.

After Carol-Lin comes home, Carol overhears her talking on the phone to Kerry, her friend. She says that if anyone in their forties has sex, it's because of abnormal hormones, or medication that has an adverse side effect. Carol-Lin adds that sex is something that belongs to beautiful young people with firm bodies.

Carol murmurs, "Their stomachs so flat that their hips can look at each other; their breasts as flat as eggs sunny side up."

Carol wonders what Kerry is saying because suddenly Carol-Lin's voice rises. "My mother," she exclaims. Then, as if she is the voice of authority, setting Kerry straight, she says, "Mom had sex a long time ago, before I was born, maybe nine months before – maybe until nine years after. She was still young then. I can't see it happening now."

Carol tries to understand Carol-Lin. She was once like her daughter, seeing an ugliness in ageing that devalued her mother. Now she feels vulnerable. She hates for anyone to visualize her as a sexual being. She can't visualize either her daughter or her mother as sexual beings.

In a surprising loss of reticence, Caroline admits that, as she knelt by a bedroom chair and pushed Carol into the waiting hands of a midwife, her pelvic bones crunched and came unlocked. She smiles wryly. "You never gave me any trouble after that. Not that Caro-Lin will give you trouble, but this is a different generation."

Carol didn't see her mother as having a future, only a past, a chastity-belted one that she wanted to inflict on her. Her mother pulled her back from her urges while Mother Nature, with the morals of an alley cat, urged her on. Her self-esteem came from resisting her "natural urges."

"Marriage is honourable and the bed undefiled, but adulterers and whoremongers God will judge," Caroline quotes the Bible to validate her sexuality in the confines of a Puritan religion that boxed sexual behavior in language such as "knew", "lay with", "went in onto."

Carol used to think that sex was something men did the same as going to the toilet and something women had only so they could do their part in contributing to the world's population: boxes coming from boxes in the form of people.

Carol is on the edge of a cliff overlooking the sea. Caro-Lin is with some guy. They are all being held hostage by a gunman. Carol is afraid. She knows that she has to make her move. She lunges forward and grabs the gun. She throws it over the cliff into the sea. Next, she is helping people in a church basement sort clothes for the poor. A shadowy form fills the doorway. She sees a gun and turns her back; a cold paralyzing fear surrounds her. She feels herself explode. A thousand shards of glass hit her in the face. Then she is whole again.

After Carol-Lin spends several weekends with Kirk's family, Carol begins to feel estranged from her as if even her thoughts have come between them.

"You don't want me to have a life," Carol-Lin retorts when she asks where she's going at night.

"Not one as small as a baby," Carol answers.

She tells her daughter, "There's a special bond with the first man you love. It's best not to pick him too early, and best not give too much to someone you only think you love. What you give you can't get back."

She's beginning to echo her mother. She resents this, even while endorsing it, the notion of sex being right under certain circumstances, a scarlet transgression under others.

She has nurtured her daughter from the moment she stirred inside her, grabbing her as she leaned down stairs, or reached for scissors. She can't stop caring for her, wanting to help her make right decisions in the face of sexually-transmitted diseases and pregnancy; love expressed ever so carefully can harm, maim, kill.

The distorted face of a pharmacist, whose eyes are staring out of his nostrils, comes close to her. He tells her that Caro-Lin can safely have sex if she comes to him. Femcon, Ma'am. That's what all the ladies are using in all colours. It gives the lady a choice. Will she, or won't she; can she or will she? Only she knows for sure. And for women over 40 a free sample of Femcon. Try them, your husband will want you to take them; middle age pregnancy causes a spread you won't want. He sees Carol's look of aversion as if he has offered her the golden calf and knows she'd like to break the ten commandments over his head. He shuts up, but not before Carol has the urge to pull his tongue out of his mouth and wrap it around his neck in a bowtie.

How can she get Caro-Lin to reveal her feelings, her fears? In her anguish Carol begrudges her daughter the calm way she wanders around. She chatterboxes on the phone and hums around the kitchen. Until now Carol has only accused her of having sex after she didn't mark an X on the calendar for July month. Carol knows she is to going to have to confront her daughter; Caro-Lin will have to respond. Time drags as she waits for confirmation or denial. Her heart begins to jump and somersault. She didn't know it could be so acrobatic. Her breathing is heavy. She sighs and opens a window to get some air. She turns; Carol-Lin's eyes meet hers. She has a look in them she's never seen before. Carol feels anger as she probes: "Answer me, yes or no."

Carol-Lin says: "Yes or no," in a deadpan voice,

"You can tell me," Carol says evenly. She imagines Carol-Lin with a swollen belly, Caroline with a great-grandchild.

"Kerry does all right. She has a baby." At last, a confirmation of the possibility.

She is in an English class. All she can see on the white chalkboard is a black question mark where a red period should be. Then a squirt of ink from her pen drops into a small hole. The circle looks white, then, maybe, pale pink. The hole is so tiny she's not sure.

She's not the first; she won't be the last. The voices are old, young, matter-of-fact platitudes. Caroline's voice leads the rest.

Brendan's silence is like a pain in her head; Carol feels alone and angry at the distance between them. She gets up and goes outside to sit on the cold steps in the silent, silvery night. She tightens her arms across her chest, pressing herself together so she won't fall apart. She shivers, and then the cold begins to hold her in its stiff embrace. She welcomes it, wanting to suffer. She feels the guilt of having hurt her daughter, the guilt of not being able to accept her daughter's sexuality, a new kind of intimacy that excludes her.

She feels an affinity with mothers everywhere who have teenage daughters. Her hurt seems to leave her body and collide with theirs in an expression of painful togetherness, and then swings back into painful isolation as she watches the young girl down the road go by. She's had a boyfriend for three years; she watched her parents' blue movies when she was ten. She's not pregnant. She just graduated. Will Caro-Lin graduate?

Kirk's car pulls into the driveway. He gets out and walks slowly towards the shed, then inside to where Carol is sitting. He is scrawny, his brown eyes wide-set in a thin face. He's a little tall for a child, yet he has the face of one. "It wasn't planned," he says slowly. His shoulders bend toward each other.

Carol wants to tell Kirk that the next time "it" starts pulsing to go squirt his love juice in the toilet, but she holds back. She doesn't want to make what he and her daughter did appear ugly and dirty.

She jumps up and goes into the house. She heads for her bedroom and falls on the bed sniffling. She is shocked by the intensity of her feelings. Thoughts keep piling up: a mass of disjointed thoughts tangled together as she searches for moral and logical order. She bites her tongue to curb its sounds of anger. She has a sudden image of Kirk's penis in a meat grinder. She immediately feels a sense of pity for him. Another surge of anger, like an electrical shock, makes her want to cry out. She feels hypocritical.

134

What gives her the right to her sexuality and her daughter and boyfriend no rights to theirs?

Carol falls asleep. *Bleeding hearts uprooted from the garden, hang over the bed; bits of turf strewn across her pillow gets inside her mouth. The house starts rocking back and forth like a rocking chair. There is no roof on the house and she can see that it's black outside. Her eyes follow twinkling stars filling the sky. They fall into red teardrops tattooing her body in exclamation points.*

It's not being in control of her daughter's life for, perhaps, the first time, a life that could affect Caroline's future as well, that ties her brain into a tight, painful knot. Despair swings like a mallet, as if demolishing the house she's built around herself.

Carol feels a wall of anger between her and her daughter after she tells her she doesn't want Kirk around. "You had a strict life; that doesn't mean you have to punish me!" Caro-Lin yells.

Punish her! Why does she think that's what it's about? Carol wants her daughter to understand a mother's responsibility to handle a situation her daughter has brought her into.

A time comes in a woman's life when she has to face more than one issue at a time, immediate ones complicated by others and, together, they create a sense of futility so strong that they threaten to destroy her. Then she has to decide how important those issues are to her identity, and if they should be allowed to threaten her future. Carol thought that reaching forty was what she was going to have to worry about, going down the hill before she got to the top. She was anticipating the worst, breasts sagging like rising dough punched down in a bread pan, and the rest of the body taking on the texture of orange peel. Not this! Women used to have babies in their forties. Now they are worrying about having their daughters' babies, as if mothers in their forties no longer have a future for themselves. She begins identifying with other women in her position – her sisters.

Carol's tongue feels like barbed wire; she's afraid of hooking her daughter's feelings on it. She clamps her lips tight.

Something breaks inside her, lets go; love fills her heart for her daughter.

She goes to bed and closes her eyes. *Carol-Lin is in a coffin. She is naked except for a chastity belt and a brank on her head like a helmet on a Christian Crusader. Carol feels the cold pressure of a key in her hand. She tries to find a lock on the brank that fits her daughter's mouth and one that fits the chastity belt that fits around her hips. There are no locks.*

Caro-Lin feels disoriented. Gradually she comes apart from who she thought she was to who she thinks she is. She becomes enveloped in who she really is: a spinster.

She doesn't belong to anyone, but herself. She laughs, an empty, echoing laugh, a laugh that runs up and down the wall of her box. She's an old spinster dreaming up lives. She's an empty box.

She raises herself to look into the mirror on her bureau, unsure of who she will see, uncertain if she's dreaming. There is no one in the mirror.

~ Nellie P. Strowbridge

Points of Light

On a handmade, crocheted doily
sits the centerpiece of my living room table:
a plate of shining brass,
holding seven candles,
cream-coloured,
slightly scented in vanilla.

Seldom are these candles lit,
seldom do I catch their hint of perfume,
for I don't want them to
melt their way to nothingness.

They were a gift:
"To Mom. Happy Birthday!"
Distance meant we weren't together
on that day; she came to visit later,
and handed me a ribbon-covered box.
I unwrapped the bright, metallic roundness,
then the candles of various sizes, one by one.
I knew they belonged on that table.
where I was bound to see them
as I carried on the daily routine.

I miss her when she's not here.
I think of her in this room, as a young child,
then as my grown-up daughter, away, perhaps,
Still always close in heart.
We have been, over the years,
each other's point of light,
beacons when needed, making our way
through the world.
I see those candles, and I see her.
I am thankful.

~ Karen Bennett

Father and Son

Father: Boy where was you at last night?

Son: I was only over to Uncle Garge's house fer a game a flop.

Father: You knows darn well, I told you to be in dis house be 9 o'clock.

Son: But fadder the hands on da clock was dere and dere, I didn't tink it was late.

Father: Well boy, dat was something to 12 and it's best you started knowing the time.

Son: Father I can't go to school and you won't help me.

Father: Why should I help you boy; I had to learn on me own?

Son: Fadder, you knows I'm farty-eight.

Father: Yes, boy, and I was farty-six when I had you.

Son: Fadder, I taught me mudder had me.

Father: Well she had you too, I s'pose.

Son: Where's me mudder anyway?

Father: I don't know boy. She left farty-six years ago when the servin' girl come here.

Son: Have I got any brudders or sisters?

Father: Don't know, me son.

Son: Den, did ya have any more servin' girls?

Father: Yes, me son; dere was four.

Son: Where's dey all at now?

Father: I don't know, me son.

Son: Why did dey leave?

Father: Well the first one left me son, cause her poor mudder was sick.

Son: What about the udders?

Father: Da next one left cause she was gittin' too fat and couldn' work.

Son: Da next one?

Father: Oh, she was getting' fat and lazy and didn't want a work.

Son: Da next one?

Father: Well, when she seen da letter I posted on da pole for a servin' girl, she walked out to the barn, put a rope 'round her neck and jumped right down the cellar hatch. Don't know for sure, but I guess she's still dere.

Son: If dis is right, I know now why you never had time to help me. I shore is glad you was busy and learned on your own. Cause you can't count the servin' girls. Fadder, don't lie, who cooked?

Father: The Missus's servin' girl across der road.

Son: I didn't know who I is, where I comes from. Now I knows. I'm farty-eight, my mudder left farty-six years ago. Ha! Ha! I'm a servin' girl's baby.

~ *Daphne Russell*

The Tailrace Clowns

Oh, this is the place, where the boozers all gather.
Some are there waiting at the break of dawn.
A few tell their spouses that they are there fishing.
We know the truth; they're just hanging around.

A few tell more lies then Joey, Danny or Dwight.
They say there's no fish and they don't wet a line.
They are there waiting, so sick they are shaking.
Hoping someone will drop by with another round.

They think they're so thrilling; they're really so chilling.
The stink of beer and sweat would knock you down.
If they broke wind together, they are ruined forever
Cause the tailrace quickly would sink right on down.

So, when you meet the guys, don't think they're all perfect.
Because we know the difference, the side that's not shown.
They are the fishing boozers; soon they'll be the losers.
They look like the sculpins, the poor tailrace clowns.

~ Daphne Russell

Every summer, fly fishermen gather to catch salmon near the old Bowater wharf off the TransCanada. Many more men and a few women go to watch the fishing, to have a chat, a cook-up and a good time.

A Poem at The Manor

I came to the Manor in September
One evening I'll always remember.
Ena came to show me around
I thought, what a nice friend I've found.

I was too excited to sleep that night.
In the morning, I was all right.
After breakfast of bacon and eggs,
I found it easier to stay on my legs.

At our table is Ena; she's not very big,
And she's not very tall
She's always happy and laughs at it all.

Next is tall Margret who is always dressed nice.
She likes plum sauce on her rice
and molasses bread with her fish.
She has her dumpling in a dish.

Shirley was sick; she had a fall.
She'd been in the hospital all this Fall.
We were expecting her back any day
Instead, she suddenly passed away

Jessie now sits in Shirley's chair.
We are happy to have her there.
Then there is me; I'm always hungry
Whenever they bring my tea.

The caregivers here are good and kind.
They're as good as you'll find,
Nurses at night, waitresses when their day shifts come.
They clean, do laundry, take care of our needs.
They are happy to be doing good deeds.

Deidre, our facilitator, has a lot to do:
Writing, spelling bees, bowling and Bingo, too.
On Wednesday she curls our hair,
Takes us to the store.
Who could ask for anything more?

At the writers' group, Deidre is very kind.
She wants us to use our minds.
There's me at the end of the table
Trying to write but hardly able
Because my fingers are so numb,
Which make me look rather dumb.
I try to write this rhyme.
I'll get it done some time.

First there is Maxine, so cute and smart.
I love her with all my heart.
Then there is Maggie
Who always says, "I can't do...."
In the end, she always comes through.

Shirley D has a great imagination.
She is always ready for an occasion.
The gem of the group,
She always has the scoop.

Wise and gentle Florence finds a lot to fill her day
Matting, quilting, and a good game of Scrabble to play.

Mary was a teacher for many years.
She is still involved in her church's affairs.
She gives a helping hand.
Whenever she can.

There's Annie G who has written many things before;
We love to see her come through the door.

My good friend, Joan, has had sciatic pain.
She broke her foot and went to the hospital again.
She missed her birthday and Christmas too.
Now's she is back as good as new.

We all loved Leah, sweet and good.
She always joined us whenever she could.
Her failing health took her away
Leaving for us a very sad day.

Last fall Joan N moved in.
A lung problem kept her on oxygen.
We became friends and used to talk.
Then she got sicker and couldn't walk.
One night she fell and they took her from here.
Now she is Palliative Care.

I live in the North Wing in room 155.
Drop in and make sure I am alive.
All the folks on this Wing are family to me.
That's the way I want it to be.

~ Myrtle Hutchings

The Light of My Life

You're always there when I need you.
You're always by my side.
I'm happy to have you with me
And show you off with pride.

From the very first time I saw you,
You looked so grand and fine.
I knew I'd never be happy
Until I made you mine.

And now that I really have you,
I'm happier than before.
I love the way you treat me.
I'll always be there for more.

I love your taste; I love your smell.
I love your contoured shape.
I love it when your glowing fire
Begins to satiate.

I often wake in the night
When all the world's at rest
And lovingly grope for you in the dark.
I'm never considered a pest.

Whenever I hold you to my lips,
And smell your fragrant scent.
I want you to stay with me always
Even when you're old and bent.

The only other thing in life
That a person of my type
Would need to make his life complete,
Is a woman warm like you, my pipe.

~ Fred Stewart
(1934 - 2007)

144

'TWIX THE SEA
& THE SKY

Home

The smell of fresh laundry drying on a clothes line.
The sound of birds singing in the early morning.
The feel of a warm breeze against your cheek.

The smell of sweet ripe berries in the midday sun.
The sound of calm waves crashing against the shore.
The feel of damp beach sand squishing between your toes.

The smell of freshly baked goods cooling on a windowsill.
The sound of croaking frogs and hooting owls at night.
The feel of the hot sun against your tanned skin.

The smell of clean fresh air when you walk outside.
The sound of chatter from a gathering group.
The feel of love in firm hugs from family and friends.

The sense of peace and tranquility all around you.
The breathtaking views as you drive across the island.
The warm smiles and common courtesy from strangers.
The overwhelming sense of pride and love for Newfoundland.

~ *Natasha Strickland*

The Cabin

Nestled in a stand of aspen
The little cabin stands.
Pots and pans line the walls
And on the porch some wood.

A rabbit trail right by the door
For hunting in the fall.
Snares and coats and snowshoes
Hang upon the wall.

A little path runs through the woods.
The boat is on the shore.
The sun is shining on the lake.
You can see it from the door.

Your rod and reel are ready
As you go out into the night.
Excitement builds within you
As the fish begin to bite.

The weekend passes in a flash
And soon you have to leave.
Another week before you're back:
Another week to grieve!

~ *Hilda King*
(1950 – 2017)

Amazing Bird

This little bird – I don't know his name – I call him Birdie, is a pretty bird. He stays in a cage here at Deer Lake Manor. One day he accidently got out of the cage and wandered away. Residents looked for him everywhere. He was missing for at least twenty-four hours.

The next day I was walking down the hall after my dinner. I decided to go down to the end of the building. When I got near, the bird was going back and forth against the window of the emergency door. Cliff P., another resident of the Manor, walked down on the other side of me.

I said, "I'm going to try to catch him; I don't care what it takes."

I went towards him as quietly as I could. When I got near, I put out my hand and, flick, he went. Well, I thought he was gone; instead, he flew across the hall and back to pitch on a small wire on my walker. Then he went over to the front bar on my walker. He didn't seem comfortable. He moved back again to the first place he landed.

I said to him, "You shouldn't have gone over there. It was too slippery for you. Stay still now." And he stayed there. He listened to me. I tell you one thing he did do: he pooped on my walker. It didn't bother me one little bit as long as he was safe.

What should I do next? I thought. I was afraid to move my walker, afraid he would take off. I decided to try it.

"Here we go birdie." All the way up the hall I talked to him in a low voice. "Stay there, birdie."

I met ladies on the way and we talked to each other. He didn't even notice it. He was looking all around as if he knew I was taking him to his cage. Was he ever cute! He was like someone enjoying a ride on his way back home.

When we reached his cage the door was open. How will I get him into the cage?

So, I turned my walker around and he was still waiting. It was amazing to see him perched upon the wire. It's a long way from the end of the building to his cage. He never tried to get away, not even once.

I pulled my walker in by the side of the cage door and into the cage he went. Cliff P. shut the door.

Thank God the bird is home. God loves the little birds. Not a sparrow falls to the ground, but God sees it. That bird went twenty-four hours without food. He was hungry and ate his bird seed as soon as he went into his cage. God came to his rescue.

That's the story of the amazing bird.

~ Annie Gillard
(1922 - 2018)

If a bird hits a window, this is an omen of death to someone close to you and your family.

Swallow

Little swallow flying high,
Up into the pale blue sky,
Wafted on its tiny wings,
While a song of love it sings.

Swooping, swaying, gliding down,
Soon alighting on the ground,
There it stands on graceful feet,
Looking for a crumb to eat.

Off it flies heading west,
There to find its little nest.
Where its babies, soft and sweet,
Wait for something good to eat.

When they're fed and settled down,
Mama then will stick around,
To make sure they're safe from harm,
Snuggled in their nests so warm.

Mother love and instinct tell
Birds protect their babies well,
Just like mothers everywhere,
They hold their babies very dear.

~ Nico LaBlanc
(Blanche Penney)
(1927 - 1989)

Chickadee

My feathery friend, the chickadee,
Decided one day that he liked me.
He perched on a branch as I came near,
For he seemed to sense there was nothing to fear.

I placed some bird seed in each hand,
And after a moment I felt him land.
He picked up a sunflower and off he flew
To return with a friend, so then there were two.
One perched on my thumb as he picked up a seed.

Goodness, how many birds was I going to feed?
They chose the sunflowers they wanted to crack
Every time that they ventured back.
Soon, all of the chickadees at our place
Were coming to meet me, face to face.

Now, when I hear them call, "Chick-a-dee-dee!"
It means, "I'm here, come and feed me!"

~ Karen Bennett

Seasons

Slob-ice caught up in whirlpools,
In waters dark and deep,
Sunshine glistening on ice caps,
On the mountains grey and steep.

Snow piled high upon the hillside,
And the valley down below,
Trees with heads bowed and trembling,
Beneath their heavy coat of snow.

What a vast expanse of whiteness,
Everything is quiet and still,
As winter spreads her snowy mantle
Over mountain, vale and hill.

Later come March winds and sunshine,
Warming up the earth below,
Rivulets of water running,
Swelling streams with melted snow.

When the snow has all but melted,
And the grass turns fresh and green,
Mother Nature with her magic
Shows us then a brand-new scene.

Daisies blooming in the meadow,
Bright white stars among the grass,
Buttercups and purple clover,
Lend their beauty as we pass.

Trees, left bare throughout the winter,
Spread their branches to the sky,
Burst into a plume of greenery
Welcoming all the birds that fly.

Sunshine rippling on the trout streams,
Birdsong thrilling with delight.
Everything bursts into blossom
In the sunshine warm and bright.

Later when the days are shorter,
Leaves turn yellow, orange and brown.
Then the farmer reaps his harvest
From the trees and from the ground.

~ *Nico LaBlanc*
Blanche Penney)
(1927 - 1989)

Drawn

I am drawn again
To the sweet-scented hills
Where the purple bell flowers
Lie in half hidden glens;
To the fern-lined trail
Where the grouse chicks flail
Their wings in deep-shaded bowers.

I am drawn again
To the mountains of mist
With their foothills of shale
Running down to the bay,
To the beaches of stone
Where ocean winds moan,
And the puffin sings to the whale.

~ Vaughn Harbin

Across the Mesh

When the Methodist minister came across the "mesh," in the first week of the cold, hungry month of March, in the Year of our Lord, 1902, Cecilia White took his visit as a sign.

Cecilia was 22 years of age and she knew that she might never leave this bleak patch of land her family called home. Other people lived far across the mesh. A different world existed.

Twice a year, her father, Jake, her brother, Michael, and their neighbour, Steven Russell, left their home, with packs of furs, treasures from shipwrecks, and smoked salmon upon their backs and headed out on the narrow path to the outside, across the barren land that separated this place from all others. They returned laden with flour, sugar, molasses, and, sometimes – Cecilia smiled at the memory, an orange for each of the family. Somewhere, across the mesh, oranges grew on trees.

That somewhere was so far away, she could only imagine such a land when she stretched out in the hay field and stared at clouds high and untouchable in the sky. Soon they'd come with scythes to slash the long grassy blades. After she arose from such stolen moments of dreaming, she carefully shook the grass and twigs from her dress and stockings, tucked her hair back into its neat bun. Her mother would never understand.

Now and then, a stranger would come accidentally upon their little circle of three families. As a child, she had pressed her ear to the keyhole of the kitchen door to listen. They thought she slept soundly in her feather bed. She heard stories of what was happening far away.

One stranger talked about trains. He said, "They're great moving boxes carrying more people than you can count. Passengers sits on seats and eats in a dining car where the tablecloths is pure white. The trains runs over tracks, lurching along clippity-clop, faster than the fastest horse."

Cecilia wondered if the train tracks were like those made by horses or hens. How could such a huge creation jump sure-footedly along tracks? Maybe the leaping and falling made the clippity-clop noise.

Strangers' stories were as unreal as the land where oranges, like wild plums, grew on trees. What was a street? How would it feel to be in a place where many unknown people roamed? And what appearance did the "Devouring Canadian Monster" wear when it threatened to take over their home and native land? Were Brits bigger and taller than the people they ruled?

At the end of the evening, her father would sigh, "Thank the good Lord we's is here to ourselfs. None of that bothers us. The Liberals, the Tories, Sir Robert Bond and Coaker, none of them matters here."

Her mother would agree, "Thank the good Lord." She'd make tea sweetened with molasses for the stranger and she'd give him (Cecilia had never seen a woman or a child appear from the mists of the mesh, from the cold of the ragged rocks of the harbour her father and Michael knew so well,) a meal of goat meat or chicken or fish with good-tasting potatoes, cabbage, turnips and pease pudding. She might even give him some cake carefully saved from Christmas past if she cared for the look of the man.

Cecilia was allowed to sit and listen in the kitchen now. Still, she hardly ever spoke. What could one say to one who came from so far away? She held onto each word, to think and savour during the long, dull hours when no one was near but her family and the Russells and the Cutlers.

Uncle Charlie Russell and Uncle Samuel Cutler (unrelated by blood, uncles by respect), had come to this land with Cecilia's grandfather fifty years past. Their wives had passed on before Cecilia came into this world. Her grandfather had died five years ago and Uncle Samuel was fading fast. They had come to this place for a reason that was never quite explained. If anyone, stranger or family, should ask why, a silence would fall in the room, so deep and dark that Cecilia had never, in all her days, seen anyone brave enough to dare to break it, to ask again, "Why did you come here?"

"What's past is past. We's is here. There's fish for us to keep and some to sell. There's food enough for all." Uncle Charlie spoke these words and Uncle Samuel nodded his head. Cecilia's father, Jake, walked to the window and stared through the wavy glass at the darkness or the sunshine. No one asked anything else.

The stranger stirred his black tea with a spoon or his finger, cleared his throat and asked a simpler question, such as, how are the fish this year, or, how does one find safe passage through the rocks of the ragged harbour?

The homeowners smiled secret smiles. "We knows the knack to it. That's all." Never would they mention the ships that sometimes beat themselves to death upon the rocks. Never would they mention the treasures washed to shore or salvaged when the sea grew quiet and the men paddled out to see what else was to be had from wreckage. Cecilia had seen bloated bodies wash ashore and sang and prayed with the others when they buried them in the seaman's graveyard in the far corner of one hay field. She had never seen a survivor from the ships, no, not once in all her 22 years. Sometimes, when the wind was high and the waves crashed, she imagined the cries of men on ships.

One stormy night, she'd put a taper in her window. She meant it as a beacon of hope, as a guide to safety. In the morning, she ran to the shore to see if a ship had blown in with the storm; she saw its sail barely breaking the surface of the waves. When the men hauled the ship in, they found water-soaked books, kegs of rum, and a ship's clock that hung in Cecilia's mother's parlour. They salvaged the wood from the broken ship and prayed over the dead bodies washing in for two more days.

After that, Cecilia lit no more candles for fear she might guide ships to their death. Yet ships, year after year, came their way driven by wild ocean currents and wind spray. It was a rare twelve-month when one vessel, or more, failed to provide for the Whites, the Cutlers and the Russells.

Thirty years ago, Jake had brought more than food back from his outside journey. Coming with him across the mesh was a woman, as tall as he, a little older, dark-skinned, sharp-nosed, bright-eyed, with a voice that never rose in anger or joy. Her name was Nancy; she fit into the little world as neatly as the tucks of homespun wool fit into her brightly coloured rugs. She made dyes for the wool from blueberries, tea, onions, beets, wild flowers and clay. If Nancy wanted a colour, she found a way to make one. Often, a stranger offered money to take one of her rugs away.

With a smile, Nancy answered, "No, thank you, sir, for asking. Perhaps your wife could make one for you." She'd draw a pattern on birch bark and pass it to the stranger. Cecilia, the only child of Nancy and Jake, had never seen her mother sell or give a rug away.

Steven Russell, Samuel's son, had found a wife, too. She was lazy and grew fat and loud over the years. Mary Russell constantly vowed to leave this place; she never did. She smacked her three children twice as hard for days after strangers vanished across the mesh. Steven left the children to his woman. And when her shrieking became too loud, he'd either find nets to mend or he'd comfort himself with rum from the swish barrel hidden in the barn.

The woman Michael brought in died in childbirth, along with her firstborn, a son. She had lasted but a year and her loss seemed to kill something in Michael, too.

Steven's sister, Ethel, had never married, and now, at 40, probably never would. She spent her hours when the work was done, playing with her niece and two nephews, heedless of the warnings from Mary that she was spoiling them and making them into hangashores. Ethel could skip rocks farther than the men. She could make a toy boat from a block of wood with a nail to hold it with a string. Her laughter mingled with the children's as they sent their boats racing in the incoming tide.

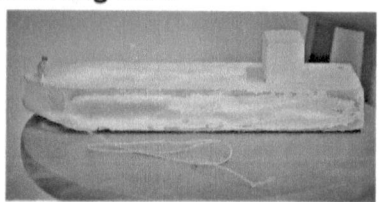

Nathaniel Cutler, Samuel's only son, had never married. He was 42 now and Cecilia had felt his eyes follow her for ten long years or more. He never went to the outside world with the other men; he never looked at the other women as he looked at her.

The men went off to check their rabbit snares one sunny winter afternoon. The women and children gathered in the Whites' home to save on fuel. They sat in the big kitchen warmed by the crackling wood stove fire. Children tossed and tumbled, practised walking with books on their heads, standing on their heads, and making odd finger shadows on the sunlit wall. Mary Russell had a pillow case in her lap and a needle and embroidery floss in her hands. That pillow case had been in her lap at times like this for five years or more. Sometimes, she stitched an x or a loop. Perhaps, if she lived another twenty years, the pattern would be completed. Ethel knitted a sweater for her niece, Euphenia – Pheenie for short. Her fingers and her clacking knit needles moved so fast they blurred. The shape of the ivory sweater emerged even as the women talked. Nancy tucked tufts of burgundy, beet-stained wool into the border of her latest rug. Cecilia had left her embroidery cotton and half-done tablecloth, her single mitten and wool, and the bag of coloured wool and mat all stacked neatly on shelves in her bedroom. She found it hard to finish anything this past year. Nothing seemed to be as it should be. Nothing seemed to work out quite right. She wanted to walk across the mesh but the men and Nancy – all besides Mary – said such a journey was not one for a woman to take.

So she stayed with the older women, the younger children, and longed for the sight of something other than wind, waves, ragged rock, and rugged vegetation. She longed for the sight of other faces, men's faces. At night, she dreamed of strangers touching her, and she blushed to think of the feelings the dreams evoked when morning light called her awake. She darned wool socks today, liking the way the wool filled in the gaping holes, making them useful but never again new. As always, Cecilia said little. She had grown up without a playmate, the single child of two quiet, loving parents. Words, spoken out loud, came hard to Cecilia. She wondered at Mary Russell. She was like a great, dark rain cloud. Words poured out of her.

The talk wandered to men. The women teased Cecilia. Ethel's time had passed. If she wished it had not, she gave no sign. Cecilia was young still.

"Ah, a stranger might come and fall for you, yet, maid," said Ethel. You's got the looks, that's for sure."

"No stranger's going to get my little maid." Nancy held the mat away from her, sizing up the evenness of the edges. "Wouldn't let him take her, I wouldn't."

"Never mind your mother, Cecilia. One of these days me and you'm, we'll go across the mesh, arm and arm, and they'll never hear tell of us again." Mary's bright eyes gleamed.

"And what's your man to do then, Mary? What's you'se going to do with the youngsters?" Ethel asked, roughly.

"Not take them with me, for sure. Ethel, you can have them all, Steven with his love of rum, the youngsters, rampsing all over you'm. You can have them all. Me and Cecilia, we's going to see the world. You'se never been outside, Ethel. You don't know how awful it is."

"Don't want to know, thank you."

"I know." Nancy's voice was low as it always was. "I don't want to go back out. Life's hard out there, Cecilia. Don't mind Mary. If she had it so good, why's she here? Answer me that Mary, why did youse come here if it's all so good out across the mesh?"

"Ah, Steven's eyes got me. His dark eyes that just about eat me all up. Lord help me, his eyes still gets to me. When he's not with the rum too long." She patted her belly. "Another one on the way. Never told you that yet, did I?"

"Shh!" Nancy whispered. "The youngsters will hear."

"No odds. They haven't got a soul to be with here. They'll have to go, Nancy, sooner or later. I'm sending them to school next year. Mom said in the letter Jake brought back she'll take them one by one provided they'll work. They're not rotting here."

"You can learn them to read and write. Mom did that with me. Nancy learned Cecilia." Ethel's hands had stopped in midair, frozen like the woodshed's outline in frosty weather. She gazed at Stanley, Pheenie and Joe guessing what animal shape might have three ears.

"How do you know there's nothing under the sun like that?" Stanley demanded. "You'ms never been anywhere outside here."

Ethel's hands collapsed. Her right fingers caressed the ringless third finger of her left hand. "Perhaps you're right, Mary, maybe it's best the youngsters get to go across the mesh. To see the world outside. Just to see."

"Theys'll grieve theyselves sick. Watch and see," Nancy predicted. "Theys'll be broken-hearted."

Cecilia kept darning, staring hard at the wool, frowning and thinking. The words of the other women stopped entering her mind. Her head was too full with her own thoughts. Her mother would never let her go. Never. She was going to stay here forever and ever and

160

never marry. No stranger stayed long enough to know it was good here. She picked up another sock. Nathaniel's sock. Since he and his dad had no woman to take care of them, and she had no man, she did her mending and his.

Cecilia looked at Nathaniel's sock. He never brought his socks over when the hole was beginning. He'd wait till it was worn right through the heel and halfway up the leg. Mending Nathaniel's sock was almost the same as knitting from scratch. Cecilia had figured out her own way of doing it, though, combining knitting and darning. Nancy said she'd never seen anything done in that strange style and never hoped to either.

Nathaniel – He looked at her the way Steven looked at Mary, the way she sometimes caught her father look at her mother when she wasn't noticing. Nathaniel didn't wake up anything inside Cecilia, not in the way her dreams did. She didn't feel a lightness when he stared at her. He was short and stocky and his hair was getting thinner and his brows were thick and almost grown together. She'd seen her mother blush, her quick shy smile at her husband. She'd seen Mary's eyes when she was with Steven, looking like a lamp was lit inside her, even while he was ducking a junk of wood she threw at him. Her eyes always held that light. Cecilia thought about Ethel. Sometimes Ethel lit with the same kind of glow when she looked at Jake; she'd turn it off and walk away fast, as if she didn't want it. And Cecilia remembered a stranger from a couple winters back who came and made Ethel laugh as much as Pheenie. She'd kept staring across the mesh. Perhaps she was waiting for him to come back. He never did and after a few months, Ethel stopped looking and went back to the way she used to be. She'd kept looking even though he'd told them about a wife and four children. The other women talked about that when Ethel was out of the room, never when she was around.

Cecilia began the repair job on Nathaniel's sock. No, much as she searched way down deep inside, she couldn't find even a flicker waiting for Nathaniel to bring it to her eyes. Still, the thought wouldn't go away after that. And, when he looked at her, she looked back.

When the Methodist minister came their way and asked if they needed a child baptized or a marriage performed, Nathaniel and

Cecilia were right there in the same room. Surely, it was a sign they should be married.

"Cecilia - " Nathaniel never asked if she'd marry him.

She knew what he meant. She nodded, yes. Then she ran from that room, the room her mother kept for meeting strangers, and she ran to her bed and she cried until the tears couldn't come any more and her handkerchiefs were all snotty.

They were married before the minister left. Nancy gave Cecilia the finest pink silk dress Jake had found in one of the shipwrecks. Mary sighed and said once she'd been small enough to wear one as pretty as that though she'd never had a chance to do so.

For ten long years, Cecilia lived with Nathaniel as best she could. She kept the Cutler house clean, kept Nathaniel's socks from ever needing her knit-darning trick; she used her mother's rugs to brighten the dark wooden floors. Nathaniel always found supper on the table and at night, when he wanted her, she never left their bed though many times she wanted to push him away. She cared for his father until he died. Nathaniel was good to Cecilia, and she to him. Cecilia never found the flicker.

Perhaps, she thought, if we could have a child, it would be different. That was not to be. They tried all the old ways remembered by her mother, Ethel and Mary − though Mary said she'd rather know how to stop babies more since she now had six. The first three had been sent across the mesh. Two were back. Only Pheenie wanted to stay away.

Mary was using a penny up inside her the last three years or so. Maybe that was working because she didn't have another on the way yet and that was a record for her and Steve. She'd got a hint that a copper coin might work that trick from a story in a magazine a stranger had left when she was in bed with her last. And she said even if it didn't work, she had a name for any child that came − a nice royal name of the face on the coin. Edward if it was a boy. Penelope, Penny, for short, if it was a girl.

The spring when Cecilia was 32, her mother sent her rooster over to "tread" Cecilia's hens. They wanted to increase their stock and have new layers and fresh poultry for the winter. One red hen was broody all the time so she was only too happy to sit on her own egg and the five from the other hens who wanted to get off the nest and go scratching for their food.

Cecilia took to going into the henhouse, an old wood shed. She couldn't stand up straight inside; the ceiling was too low. The smell of the manure stung her nose and made her eyes water. Even so, she'd crouch and talk away to the red broody hen who hadn't been allowed to hatch a brood before.

"We's not taking you'ms eggs away this time, Reddy. This time, you'se is goin' to get to see you'ms little chicks. Little yellow fuzzy balls, on the first, they is. You'ms going to love them." Cecilia cleaned out the henhouse and put in fresh straw every day. She'd collect the eggs from the other hens and murmur, "Funny how some don't care about their young." She'd sigh as she used those eggs for baking and for breakfast.

The women frowned when they saw her go to the woodshed every day and stay longer than she had to. She had it so clean it did not smell as bad now Still, a henhouse was not a place for a grown woman to go. The men didn't notice and when the women talked to them, they laughed it off.

Mary called Nathaniel over to her fence one day. "You should keep an eye on Cecilia, Nathaniel. She's acting odder than a missing sock."

Nathaniel's broad black eyebrows came together and his forehead wrinkled right up to where his hair used to be. "Leave she be, Mary. Cecilia's not hurting a soul. You'se knows how picky she is. My house is so clean a fly won't flutter in and there's not a thing left to fix now. She thinks the chicks are her babies."

"That's what I thinks! And if I was you, I'd be thinking what that was all about. She needs a chick of her own, Nathaniel, my son. Maybe I'll have to send Steven over."

Nathaniel turned sharply and walked away but not before Mary saw the colour flood right over his whole face. She laughed out loud and wished she could share the joke with someone. Steven would slap her for it. Ethel would frown. Nancy wouldn't hear a word against anyone. Would Pheenie listen and laugh? Mary wasn't sure. And it had been a long time since a light-hearted stranger had come by.

When the chicks hatched, all except one, Cecilia brought them around to show them off, though chicks hatched every year and they were all much the same. The women worried and the men laughed off her pleasure.

The chicks grew quickly. The rooster, she called Ben. The hens were Regina, Delilah, Bessie, and Marcy.

"You shouldn't name them," Nancy warned one day when she watched Cecilia laugh as she scattered bread to her hen family. "Them is not pets, not like dogs they haves outside. Thems'll lay for a time and then you'll have them for dinner."

Cecilia's face paled. She flung the last of the bread in a pile and ran away from her hens, away from her mother, out into the hay field where she lay and cried. She stared up at the blue sky through her tears and vowed, "Them is not going be stuffed down Nathaniel's gullet. Them's not."

The summer passed and winter set in. Cecilia still talked to her hens and they followed her and gathered around her as though they knew they were hers.

One freezing winter day, Cecilia saw Nathaniel sharpen his axe. A coldness gripped her from way inside where the flicker never did begin. The goat meat was gone. The winter caribou hunt was not yet successful, and, Nathaniel did love his meat.

He saw her watch the axe take on its shining edge. His eyes grew soft as he saw her frightened gaze. "I'll only take one."

His words whirled within her head. "I'll only take one."

Which one? Not Ben. They needed him for treading. Fluffy Marcy? The fighter, Bessie? The one who always came to meet her first, Regina? Or the frailest, the one she fed on the sly before the others came, Delilah? "No!" The word began softly, grew louder, higher, till her mother came running to see what hurt her daughter. She saw the axe, Nathaniel's wondering gaze. Nancy knew, as mothers do, what was wrong.

"Leave the chickens be for now, Nathaniel. I's got a good pot of bottled rabbit stew on my stove right now, enough for you'se two. Come on now."

Cecilia ate her stew. She went home with Nathaniel. For the first time in the long years of their marriage she turned away when he wanted her.

She waited until his sleep was sure, until his snoring shook the walls. She put on her warmest clothes and took a brin bag from the lower pantry shelf. She crept to the hen house, picked up the squawking chickens, one by one, whispering softly, "You'ms going to be fine. Not going down Nathaniel's gullet. You'se not got to worry. Youm'll be all right in a little while."

She left the shelter of the three houses and their buildings clustered under the shining, haloed, crescent moon. She headed out across the frozen mesh with her chickens cuddled, wriggling, against her breast.

She didn't notice when the wind began to blow powdered snow around her legs, when it picked up speed and clouds covered the moon, or when snow began falling faster and faster. She felt cold, everywhere but where she held the chickens. They kept her warm. Her toes, her legs, her whole body, where the chickens were not held, became colder, colder, tingling cold. Her shoulders grew weary, her steps slower. She wondered when she'd see the trees where oranges grew. They would be strong trees to hold such large and shining fruit, even if they slept in this winter wind. The snow made seeing hard and she felt tired now, so tired. She'd have to take a spell; she could go no further this cold and snowy night.

Cecilia lay down on the frozen mesh, chickens cuddled into the circle of her body. She fell asleep, smiling at the squawking chickens, murmuring, "Sh, sh. You'se with me now."

They found her in the second week of April in the year of our Lord, 1913, curled up with her chickens in a shape that could not be straightened. Nancy wrapped her in fine linen from last year's wreck. Nathaniel dug a hole as deep as he could in the spongy spring mesh. They prayed and sang a hymn, and buried Cecilia in the mesh, cuddled into her chickens.

~ Deborah Hedd

Blindness

I feel the darkness closing in,
Daylight slowly fade,
My blinded eyes cannot see
The beauty God has made.

I'm told the sky is grey or blue,
With fluffy clouds so white.
Summer leaves and grass are green,
And make a lovely sight.

The silver moon and stars at night,
The golden sun by day,
Shine down upon the flowers
In all their bright array.

Who can describe to someone blind,
What darkness is – or light?
How can you tell what colour is
To someone without sight?

The sightless one can tell by touch
What beauty means to her,
A mother's face with gentle smile
A kitten's soft, warm fur.

The warm sun shining from above,
The gentle splash of rain,
The cooling winds of winter
Bringing ecstasy or pain.

The sounds of nature waking up
With bird song sweet and clear,
The smell of something cooking
That is wafted on the air.

The joyful sounds of children,
As they go about their play,
And the common, everyday things
That we cherish on life's way.

~ *Nico LaBlanc*
Blanche Penney)
(1927 - 1989)

Hearts That Give Heed to The Sea

Clarion is the call of the cliffs
Of the sea as they speak to me.
Salt is the taste of the wind on the beach
As the ocean seduces me.
Pure are the thoughts that arise within
As my heart responds to the call
Of the waves that tantalize the rocks,
Then break against the wall.
Stronger each day my soul seems to grow
As I gaze upon the sea.
And wiser and truer the hearts of my friends,
Hearts that give heed to the sea.

~ Vaughn Harbin

"Leave Me These!"

The fragrance of roses dipped in dew,
The wonder of infants, mild and new.
Ruby-lipped children who laugh as they play
In soft black turf and newly mown hay.
A peaceful stroll on a summer's eve,
An innocent look I can believe.
Cantering horses on stone-walled lanes.
Whispering white oaks and weather vanes.
Shimmering lakes 'neath an azure sky,
Hearts that give love, but never ask why.
Moss-covered tree trunks and fallen leaves,
Misty-eyed maidens, youths on their knees.
Eyes of a lover true and wise,
Sun-kissed diamonds in disguise!
Soft brown curls in a gentle breeze….

Ah! Take all else – leave me these!

~ Vaughn Harbin

Our Home

When the day's sun shines
in all its splendour above the herring gulls cry.
The silence of dawn moves along,
signaling the onset of winter weather
the return of ferry boats
delivering the unknown to the known.
Here the sun remains over the land
when one has gone as far as one is able
beginning in the west ending out east,
gaining ground while Earth makes her rounds.

Our people since Confederation's time
the year of 'forty-nine
work from our need and culture
steeped like a good cup of tea
in five centuries of history
abiding by the coastline rules
shaped by the mighty land
bashing seas under watchful sea gull flocks.

The Labrador land abundantly blessed with the very best rivers
fed by brooks, realized dreams for people who love the land and
sea.
Complemented by this island in the sea.

People come to see the icebergs birthed in the north,
Come to skirt our shores.
A photograph never captures such an awesome sight.
Icebergs, finding their own way like the clouds in the sky.
Touching each other at times.
Captured by such a sight,
I look up, down, then all around.

Winter lets go and spring takes hold,
the days get longer,
the world shines like a new found pearl,
her strength rises like a cresting wave,
northward from the West, onward to Cape Spear.

Come, see the gift God gave us:
the north land and sea.
Watch the rays of the sun pale the sky,
ride the cresting waves to the shoreline
of our home: Newfoundland and Labrador.

~ *Dana Cole*

The Vision

Searton, Codroy Valley 1910

One summer evening, Teresa O'Quin, an eleven-year-old and her sister were helping their mother around the house and preparing supper. They were expecting the O'Quin men and other men to return soon.

The father, a typical farmer/fisherman and a seasonal worker with forestry, had gone out on the water with four other men; one was his brother. There were uneasy looks from the families on land as the day progressed. The weather had turned sour with high winds.

Around 5 o'clock, Teresa's mother asked her sons, Richard and Andrew, fifteen and sixteen, to go out to the barn to help the men with their "catch".

Moments before, Teresa, her mother and other members of their family, had seen the men with their horse and wagon loaded with barrels of fish, come up the roadway; the men were heading towards the barn to sort their "catch".

Richard and Andrew went to the barn, but they soon came back saying, "No one is there."

The men had not come up with the horse and wagon.

Teresa and her mother left their house and walked down the lane to a relative's home. Teresa's aunt was also busy preparing supper for her husband. She, too, had seen the men with the horse and wagon go up the roadway. The women were bewildered and concerned. They rushed down to the ocean area. They quickly realized that the boat was not tied to the wharf or anywhere along the shoreline. Several men had already launched their large boat and were preparing to go out to rescue fishermen from a boat that had capsized in the high winds.

Onlookers began gathering by the shoreline concerned that it might be their men who were in trouble. Teresa was sent back up to the house to get her brothers in case they were needed. When she returned, she saw the larger boat returning and heard a commotion aboard.

As the boat neared the wharf, there were calls for someone to bring blankets and light the stoves.

The battered O'Quin men were lifted ashore and taken to the nearest homes.

Teresa shivered as she heard a man say, "Your father drowned but we revived him. The other men are in bad shape, too."

The community worked together to get the men inside, warmed and cared for.

Teresa's uncle told how their boat, with its load of fish, had swamped and capsized, sending the men into the cold water. Hours had passed by the time they were rescued.

When times were compared, people realized that Teresa and her mother had seen the men returning at the same time that the boat overturned.

The wives of two of the men insisted that they had seen the men with the wagon and horse go up the roadway. Knowing that the winds were extremely strong, they had been quite relieved to see the men safe and sound.

Later that night, as the men regained their strength, their version of events were touching and eerie. Teresa's father, a terrible swimmer, had fought to stay alive with his brother and the other men, fighting the cold and the waves as long as he could. He finally prayed that God would take care of his family as he gave in to exhaustion. It was then that he felt as if he were in a dream in which he and the other men were heading up the roadway.

His dream had somehow connected with the families waiting for their men to come home.

~ Told to Greg Alexander, a descendant.

The Line 'Twix The Sea and The Sky

I think the sea has a hold on the soul
Of everyone who's lived close by
There's the lull of the waves
The screech of the gulls
And the line 'twix the sea and the sky.

In coves and the bay
Whales frolic and play
And icebergs get lost in the fog
There's salt in the air
And the dampness is there
But it's so much better than smog.

The wind calls out to me
As it batters the sea
And I whisper my reply
I whisper my reply
As I drift 'twix the sea and the sky.
I drift 'twix the sea and the sky.

~ Jean Legge Hiscock

Ocean

I am an Ocean, the Pacific Ocean,
The strongest ocean in the world.
I am as blue as the sky on a hot summer day.

I can do anything I want, throw around
Ships like rag dolls.
Some days I unleash my fury,
Make tidal waves, destroy houses and
Even surf boarders.

There's two things I am afraid of,
Oil tankers spilling oil all over me and making
Me dirty,
Or a year of constant sun to dry me up.

I am a home for man and creatures such as
Whales, fish, sharks, sea gulls and dolphins.
I am the great and mighty Pacific Ocean.

~ *Desmond Russell*

"A green Christmas foretells a fat graveyard."

The Gulch

Words on Wings/ The Road

When you arrive at that point just over the crest
On your way to Trout River looking out towards the west
You see this vista of Tableland glory
With orange-coloured rocks "quite a geological story"
That tells of Earth's mantle from way deep below
That rose skyward 500 million years ago
And gave us a sight that is truly beholding
And continues each day as if it's still unfolding.

It's a sight to be seen
In a land that is rocky and rough, yet pristine.
And that section of road, "the Gulch," you know
Can be saddled in winter with drifts of snow
Twelve feet or higher. It's hard to believe
It's true! No need to deceive.
Take warning from me if you travel this highway
Don't take the attitude that, "I'll do it my way!"
If locals tell you not to travel this path,
Better to listen than get caught in the wrath
Of Mother Nature's scowling winds and weather
Only to think that things will get better
Because they won't! The Gulch will get blocked
While your car with snowdrifts around you gets socked
In with pounding winds and wheels bogged down
And your life is at risk 'cause you didn't stay in town
Where there's always a meal and a place to stay.
Yes, you know that's certainly the Newfoundland way.
So beware of the Gulch, Autumn, Winter and Spring
And never take this road on a prayer and a wing!

~ Mike Madigan

Baby Tree

Across the valley
Over the mountain
Lies beauty:
The land so green
The sea so blue
The air so pure
And true
The mountains so high
The sand so soft
And in the middle of it all
The green
Small
Short
But strong
Baby tree.

~ *Terri Hayden (Moores)*

Timber Moose

Majestic in his forest land
Well hid among the timber stands,
My moose has seen me first and fled
Fearing a blast of my shotgun lead.

Through the tangle of roots and trees
Stirring the nest of flies and bees,
The powerful beast is gone from sight.
I pant and follow and ponder my plight.

I curse the branch that whips my jaw,
The stinging of my lips rubbed raw,
The sucking, pulling, watery bog,
An ever elusive tripping log.

My heart is pounding loud and fast
For I have found my moose at last,
Outside my zone, calm and still
Nibbling browse, eating his fill.

The need for steak rattles my gut.
I long for a sizzling slice of his butt.
He stands tall and proud and seems to gloat −
The most civilized animal of us both.

~ *Jean Legge Hiscock*

177

The Lovely Spud

The little spud
With his eyes full of mud
Lay on the ground all alone.
The carrots there
All formed so fair
Looked at the little spud.
They said, "My dear, look over there
That filthy one do see.
We'll soon be gone in a salad so gay
To crown the table so proud
For Ladies and Gents
With lots of sense
To dine and eat their full."

The poor little spud
Said not a word
Till one fine day
A little boy
Was walking with his dad.
He saw the spud with mud in his eye.
He said, "Daddy, dear, come over here.
Some crispy potato chips we'll fry."

~ G. M Legge

To A Chick

Teeny, tiny ball of fluff
Trying to get your belly stuffed
Never know when you've had enough
Teeny, tiny ball of fluff

Teeny, tiny ball of fluff
Do try to get your belly stuffed
And when I see you've had enough
I'll have your little life all snuffed

~ *Jean Legge Hiscock*

The Great White Hunter

The great white hunter made his plans,
To stalk his prey across the land,
Packed grub and beer, adjusted scope,
Of bagging a bull moose.

With painted truck and top-notch gear,
With painted face and army wear,
With keen ability to shoot,
With hunting savvy there to boot,
The bull was in the bag.

Day after day the hunt went on,
Starting at the crack of dawn,
Through morning, noon, and into dusk,
The days flew by and still no luck
In bagging a bull moose.

The man was honest all the time,
Obeyed the laws and rules and signs,
No hunting 'fore the sun comes up,
From helicopter or his truck-
He had integrity.

But time was drawing to a close,
And panic moved from head to toes;
To face the boys would be pure hell,
With neither macho tale to tell,
And brag about at work.

The last day came, just one more try
To keep his manliness alive,
To ward off the embarrassment
Of failing in his last attempt
To bag a big bull moose.

He pondered life, its pros and cons,
And why a moose won't come along;
He stopped to sit and rest a while,
But settled down upon a pile
Of buttons, warm and fresh.

Smeared up with dung, a curse he said,
But then a thought came to his head,
Fresh buttons mean the moose is near!
Excited, he picked up his gear
And went to bag his moose.

With hope renewed, the man did creep
On hands and knees without a peep,
'Til out there standing on a mish
He saw his prize! He'd get his wish!
And bag a big bull moose.

The big bull stood there, proud and sure,
Sporting twenty point or more,
A dream come true, there was no doubt,
The boys would surely talk about
The man who bagged the bull.

He aimed to kill it clean and quick,
But then he heard a sickening click;
At once he knew, of all the luck,
He'd left the bullets in the truck!
Goodbye to the bull moose.

The hunter stood there in defeat,
Dejected, he tried not to weep,
For now, he knew that all was lost,
In no way could he face the boss
And all the boys at work.

181

BUT:
The bull moose, too, was hurt by fate,
'Cause up to now he'd had no mate.
He ached all over - with good reason.
It was past the ruttin' season,
And he had struck out cold.

Like the man, the bull was beat,
Lonely, lost, he felt defeat.
He sensed that nature turned her back.
He had no choice but face the fact,
He would not sire a calf.

But chance was yet to intervene.
A gust of wind came on the scene,
Went past the man and to the bull,
Who stood there with his instincts full
Of need to reproduce.

Excited by this different scent,
The moose turned 'round and then he went
After the man, who wondered what
Had caused the bull to turn and trot
Towards his hiding place.

But then he knew, to his dismay,
Just why the moose had turned his way.
"The dung," he said, "has caused a stink
Which has made the bull to think
That I'm the cow he needs!"

With terror coursing through his blood,
The hunter ran through trees and scrub.
His mind was filled with just one prayer,
A fate much worse than death.

He kept the pace o'er bog and fen,
Spurred on by his adrenalin,
But still the moose gained on the man,
Who knew he'd better get a plan
Or kiss the world goodbye.

Then up ahead he saw a way
To save himself and make his day.
A little further then he stopped,
For just beyond there was a drop
Of twenty feet or more.

The moose kept charging, making moans,
Spurred on by his testosterone.
And as the man stood at the cliff,
The bull kept heading for the whiff
Of buttons, warm and fresh.

With passion great, the moose barged on,
Regardless of what lay beyond,
And with one bold and mighty leap
He knew that he would soon repeat
The yearly ritual.

The hungry bull soared through the air;
The man stayed calm, he had no fear,
For just in time, with great aplomb,
He jumped aside; the moose flew on
And tumbled down the cliff.

The bull was dead, the man was blessed,
And soon the animal was dressed
And out aboard the pickup truck.
The hunter thankful for his luck
In bagging his bull moose.

But, though he had a trophy rack,
He really had much more than that;
For in addition to his prize,
He had a tale to tell the boys,
And brag about at work.

~ *David Elliott*
(1946- 2001)

Soup

Hens
Without their feathers
Make good soup
So do the necks of turkeys
And the legs
And flesh
Of cows and moose.

I like soup
Birds, cows and moose
Don't.

~ *Jean Legge Hiscock*

Ashley the city cousin is visiting Madison out in the Bay. Along comes a pig, ordinary-looking enough, except for one thing, it had a wooden leg.

Ashley:	Why does that pig have a wooden leg?
Madison:	That is one special pig. Why, it hauled my grandson right out the ocean, saved his life.
Ashley:	Wow. Did he lose his leg doing that?
Madison:	Nope. And that pig unlatched the barn door and saved ten horses from burning to death when the barn caught fire.
Ashley:	Did the pig lose its leg in the fire?
Madison:	Nope.
Ashley:	Madison, why does that pig have a wooden leg?
Madison:	It's like this, cousin. When you have a pig that's so special, well, you don't eat it all the one time.

Freedom

Over the rocks and over the sand
Lady played and Lady ran.
"Free at last," she seemed to say.
"No chain around my neck today."

Across the beach she ran with ease
Up the trail and through the trees.
She sniffed the ground along the way,
Free to have some fun today.

Faster than the speed of sound,
She chased her tail 'round and 'round.
She spied a squirrel up a tree
Couldn't get to it, but Lady's free.

Hours later she trudged in the door.
Ever so tired, she flopped to the floor.
She looked at me as if to say,
"Thank you for my freedom today."

~ Hilda King
(1950 - 2017)

IMAGINE THERE'S NO LIMIT

A Toast to Trucks

Here's to the truck that carries my groceries,
tea and fruit and meat.
Here's to the truck that brings heating oil
to warm wintry-cold hands and feet.

Here's to the truck that brings gasoline
from such a long distance away.
Here's to the truck which I can't drive
with fuel prices that soar every day.

Still, I'll raise my glass high in the air,
and give the trucks a mighty loud cheer.
'Tis only water I'm toasting with now,
'cause I can't afford no beer!

~ Karen Bennett

Choices

Road safety is paramount for government and local communities. We determine our fate. The body follows the line, it all depends on us, yes, it all depends on what we choose to do. It will be what we want it to be.

If no speed limits are broken, please God, we will reach our destination. Fight the good fight, given the chance. Choose life and liberty or there could be bars between you and the freeway. The kids need to see how it ought to be; you may be ticketed because you put the pedal to the mat, it is not the end; you'll have another chance.

You can make a comeback. That's the essence of grace. The person we glimpse in the corner of our eye when they pass is the one who should determine that we do what's best. No one should be exempt. It's never too late; we can start right from the gate. Let your engine run in a way to make sure you'll make it back home, yes, sweet home.

Back in the day, the horses' hooves thundered across the land. Control the burn, let the kids live and learn how they should act by what you do. ***Learn the rules of the road. They are not to be broken***; The plan is the same for everyone. Every time we get behind the wheel we must stay left of the white line and right of center. The rules are not to be broken; it's a study in contrast; staying between the lines is paramount. Obey the speed limit even when people fly by in downpouring rain, they are a danger to anyone near them. Slow down. It is the best thing you could do.

We're only human, we are supposed to make mistakes and we must learn our limits, or it will be only a matter of time before we see the red and blue light in the rear-view mirror.

When it comes to the law, in a manner, it's three strikes and you are out. If you accumulate 12 demerit points, (speeding 10 to 20 kilometres over the limit 3 times) you lose your licence.

I once heard someone say: learn from other people's bad behavior rather than misbehaving, yourself. When someone is learning to drive they usually take their time. Other people go wild with the pedal under their feet once they have their licence.

Fortunately, we eventually come to respect the laws of the road. I am one who learned the hard way to do what was best,

A woman helped me see the light and start doing things right. She is my most precious gift. She calmed my spirit and my need for speed went away. Now she drives and I enjoy the scenery, answering the phone, reading the map, and she follows my lead. I get joy out of knowing how much she loves to drive. Her mom and dad are proud because she did as she was taught to do, respecting the laws of the road.

Nowadays, the only time I experience speed is when I play my racing video game, and that's plenty of speed for me. That may sound silly, but it works.

Nighttime driving is different from day time driving; our field of vision is different. You should look out your side window to see how fast you're really going. Following the laws of the road depends on our perspective. Being mindful of other people doesn't happen automatically; it requires consideration and determination. We are known by what we don't do, as well as by what we do.

When we are behind the wheel, we are not alone. We should be aware that our actions affect those with us and those on the street: other automobiles and pedestrians. Playing by the rules is essential to the safety of everyone. This is true when we are behind the wheel on the road. It is also true as we find our way along the other highways of life.

~ Dana Cole

My Trip

My trip to the States was a memorable one,
With lots of driving and lots of sun.
On August the fourth we left our home,
It was 4:15 AM when we started to roam.
We arrived in Port aux Basques at seven o'clock,
The Caribou waiting at the dock.
We got the boat and had something to eat.
It was so early and I was quite beat.
When the boat finally docked on the other side,
We got in our van and went for a long ride.
We drove from North Sydney all the way to Saint John,
To the Colonial Inn where we stayed until dawn.
Up the next morning and off to the border,
all of our ID's checked and in order.
We drove all day stopping to shop and to eat,
With our air conditioner on so we could stand the heat.
Old Orchard Beach was our target that day.
When we arrived we had no place to stay.
People had told me that the beach was a blast,
That the pier would be wonderful and the rides would be fast.
This was a whole bunch of lies.
The only thing wicked about the beach was the guys.
After one short ride we were on our way,
Looking for another place to stay.
We finally found the Drake Motel.
We settled in and all was well.
We were up early the next morning ready to roll.
We found beautiful York Beach and went for a stroll.
While there, Cheezies to the sea birds I fed,
Then back on the road for shopping ahead.
The shopping was great and I bought lots of stuff,
Would it fit in the van; would we have room enough?
We drove down through Maine continuing our quest.
When we got to Massachusetts we quickly turned west.
We rushed through New Hampshire, running late,

Then we drove 'cross the border to New York State.
And then on to Marilyn and Jim's place.
It was comfy and cozy and had lots of space.
It was built in 1840 and filled with antiques,
With the original floor boards. Oh, how they did creak!
While in Ballston Spa we did lots of fun things,
We visited the race track at Saratoga Springs.
We swam in a pond and went for walks.
We relaxed and enjoyed long late night talks.
We went to Vermont to look at some sights;
The scenery was beautiful to my delight.
While visiting we went shopping for antiques.
The store was big we could have stayed for weeks.
Visiting Howes Caverns was the highlight of my stay,
The exciting walk and the boat ride made my day.
In case you don't know what Howes Caverns are,
They are dark eerie caves underground real far.
Now my Mom she really loves to sew,
So to sewing and quilting shops we had to go.
After shopping at the last one we looked for somewhere to stay.
The only place with an empty room was 300 miles away.
We drove and drove without luck or hope.
We were tired and hungry. How would we cope?
We continued to drive through the dark and rain,
What would we do? It was driving me insane.
While stopped in a road block; we asked the police for advice.
He talked to us calmly and was very nice.
He said we could park in the police lot till morn;
It was no hotel and it wasn't too warm.
We survived and actually got some sleep.
It wasn't too comfortable but it was sort of neat.
The next day we went shopping again.
It was a beautiful day, not too hot with no rain.
After shopping and eating we were on our way,
At the Machias Motor Inn was where we would stay.
The place was great with a really nice pool.
I swam the whole while; it was pretty cool.

The next day we crossed the US-Canada border,
Once again making sure all of our ID's were in order.
We made it across with no problem at all.
We were behind schedule and had no time to stall.
Once again we drove a long way.
We had to catch the ferry early the next day.
That night I stayed with my uncle in Baddeck.
After all that driving I was a wreck.
We had to get up early to make the boat back home.
I was tired and cranky and my hair was uncombed.
After the boat finally got to the dock,
I knew that we were back on the Rock.
We got in the van and I felt kind of sad;
It was over, the best holiday that I ever had.
I will always remember that trip to the States;
The fun we had and the stores that were great,
The walks and the talks and the very long drive,
The sun and the heat and all the wicked guys,
The beaches and food and the people we met,
I wished that the trip wasn't over yet.

Road Trip: 1997

~ Sarah-Lynn Bussey

"Stay where you're to 'til I comes where you're at."
Don't go anywhere until I get there. Wait for me.

Fear Aboard the Airplane

Susan Ashley, a tall, slim, brown-eyed young woman had promised herself that she would never fly in a plane. Every time she imagined herself flying, she'd feel a sudden electric shock in her stomach, as if she were falling through the door or window and plunging toward the earth.

Although Susan had resolved not to do it, she did eventually travel by air when she was twenty-three.

One beautifully warm spring night, as she sat outdoors on the patio, a soft breeze made the slightest sound in the trees. A full moon began to rise above hills. She looked up at the sky, adorned with twinkling stars, and thought, "What if I decide to spend my vacation with my relatives on the mainland, how would I travel?" She knew that, if she went by ferry and train, she would spend six of her fourteen holidays in travelling time. By air it would only take sixteen hours. "I'm probably one of the world's greatest cowards," she thought.

The air was now cooler. She felt cold and tired. She got up and stopped by her apartment door for a moment before going in. She went to bed and lay awake for a long time watching moonbeams and pondering. Tomorrow, she would have to decide. She closed her eyes and fell asleep.

In the morning, with the sun shining in her room, she put on her pretty pink dress, fastened with a pin made of jade and stood before the mirror looking at herself, pleased with how she looked. She locked the apartment door; then she walked down to the street where people were already hurrying to their jobs. She thought of calling her relatives in Toronto. She decided to make reservations first.

During lunch hour, she walked slowly through the bright sunshine on Main Street to the restaurant. As she entered, she saw her friends sitting at the far end of the room. They waved to her. She picked up a tray, placed her usual cold sandwich and milk on it, then walked quickly across the room to join them. Their conversation was about vacations. "Where are you going for your vacation, Susan?"

asked Jane, a buxom young woman with blue eyes and long dark hair.

"I've been thinking about going to Toronto. I'm terrified when I think about flying," Susan said. Each girl told of her experience when flying.

Katie, a petite blonde with brown eyes, said, "It is as safe in a plane as in a car or boat."

With the help of her friends' encouragement, Susan made reservations with Air Canada.

At last, she was at the airport. The taxi driver carried her bags in and put them down at the check-in counter. Susan looked bright and excited, her blonde hair curling softly around her face. Her flowered, white dress made her look cool and fresh.

While she waited for the flight to be called, she looked at the crowd of people sitting or standing around talking; some smoked cigarettes; one man filled his pipe from his tobacco pouch; other people stood by the window, watching as planes landed and passengers got off.

She stood for several minutes wondering if these people were as composed as they looked. Then the final announcement was made for passengers to leave at Gate 11 for points as far as Toronto.

She walked with the crowd to the plane and went up the stairs, and casually passed her boarding pass to the stewardess, as if she had done this many times before. She walked into the plane and sat in a seat near the window opposite a wing. A stout, elderly man, wearing a black business suit, sat in the seat next to her. He placed his hat on the rack, settled down and began to read his newspaper. The sign up front read, "Fasten Your Seat Belts." Susan fastened her seat belt and kept tugging at it as if she would never get it tight enough.

Leaning back, Susan heard the roar of the engines and felt enveloped in fear. She tried hard not to look out the window as the plane started to taxi down the runway. She didn't want to know when it left the ground. If she didn't see it leave, the fear might go away. Curiosity always got the best of her and she slowly turned her head and watched as the plane wheeled around and made a fast run for take-off. As the plane rose higher, her heart beat very fast for a while; then she felt as if it was going to stop beating completely.

The stewardess, immaculate in her blue uniform, offered Susan a magazine. She flipped through the pages, trying hard not to look outside. The sun was pouring in through the window. After putting the magazine in the pocket on the back of the front seat, she looked out and saw the white, fluffy clouds spread out as far as the eye could see. She thought to herself: "How wonderful it would be if I stepped out and walked around!"

Suddenly she imagined herself falling through the fluff. She drew her breath quickly and put her hand to her chest, holding herself tightly. She looked at the man across the aisle. He didn't see her look of fear. The stewardess pushed a food cart down the aisle and served lunch. Susan tried to concentrate on the food.

After a while, a pleasant voice said, "May I have your attention please?"

Susan lurched in her seat. Her heart raced.

The voice continued, "We are going to land with a 20-minute stop in Halifax."

The void beyond the plane's window was a magnet, pulling at her. She looked down at the earth and tried to find a good place where the plane could land in case of an emergency. The plane was flying over farms and the land resembled carpets or patchwork quilts, with squares of green and brown. In the rural centers, tiny, toy cars moved along the streets. The view distracted her.

"Thank you, God, we are safe," Susan prayed. She remained on the plane, trying to pacify her fear and be reasonable about flying the remainder of the way to Toronto.

Susan fastened her seat belt for the take-off from Halifax. There had been no mishap thus far, so she should have no cause for anxiety the rest of the way. A short distance from Halifax the plane ran into dark clouds. Susan was horrified to see flames shooting out from the engine. She turned and touched the man next to her, her voice shaky: "The engine is on fire."

He turned quickly and looked out the window at the engine, then back at Susan. Smiling, he said, "The engine is not on fire, it's a turbojet; you only see the flame while in dark clouds or at night."

Without another word, he tipped his seat back as far as it could go and became engrossed in a paperback novel, until they landed in Montreal to change planes. Her mental anguish was now centered on which of the many planes she was supposed to board.

When the announcement was made for passengers to leave by Gate 9 for Toronto, Susan recognized some of the people who were on the other plane. She stood in line with them, never letting them out of her sight until they were on the plane leaving for Toronto.

Things went well for the remainder of the flight. A young woman about her own age with green eyes and long, straight black hair, sat in the next seat. They found so much to talk about that the time passed quickly until the plane reached Malton Airport. Then Susan collected her luggage.

Her vacation was over too soon and she was back at the airport again, waiting in line to board the plane and return home to Newfoundland. She looked around to wave goodbye to her relatives. Then the gate opened, passengers moved outside and she felt really pleased with herself. She would not be afraid again.

On the plane, in the seat beside her was a young woman with her small boy. When the plane gathered speed for take-off, the young woman leaned forward and said, "I'm terrified."

Susan turned to her, "You have no need to be scared. How far are you going?"

"I'm going to Labrador City to join my husband." She made a little movement of her hands and twisted a little in her seat. "I've never been on a plane before."

Susan comforted her. "I was so frightened on my way up from Newfoundland. We really do not have anything to fear. I feel fine now."

Soon the plane landed at Dorval Airport. Then, because of a hurricane along the Atlantic Province, all planes were grounded. Arrangements were made for passengers to stay at a nearby hotel.

The next day, the plane got as far as Sydney, Nova Scotia and was grounded again. Everybody stayed in the terminal all night. At midnight they were told that the flight out to Newfoundland had room for only thirteen passengers. At 1:00 AM Susan was told she was on the list and that it was very stormy over the Atlantic Ocean, but that the plane would fly above the storm.

Somebody said that the best place to sit was up front near the pilot's cockpit. At 1:30 AM, they all walked silently out of the terminal and as soon as the stewardess saw her boarding pass, Susan stepped quickly inside and sat in the very first seat. Seat belts were fastened and the plane roared down the runway and took off into the dark, stormy clouds. It was quiet inside. Some of the people were either sleeping or reading. Susan felt curiously relieved by her lack of fear.

Suddenly, the plane began to bounce about. Then it dropped so quickly, Susan felt her heart flutter alarmingly. She looked about in dismay. It dropped again and her stomach twisted in knots. After a while things seemed to be back to normal.

Suddenly the young man seated opposite her said, "Look, smoke!" He pointed across at the floor.

Susan took a deep breath. She walked cautiously up to the cockpit without saying a word. The pilot explained what was happening.

She edged back to her seat and assured the young man, "That's vapour. It usually comes through the seams in a storm."

At last, about one and a half hours later, the plane landed safely at Stephenville Airport in Newfoundland.

Susan left the plane, her initiation to air travel completed.

~ *Edith Johnston*
(1917 - 1998)

This story was written at a time when passengers could choose their own seats and when smoking was allowed in airports.

Woman of Colour

"Canada is full of other people, people of colour,"
I heard a CBC commentator say.
"Michaëlle Jean is a woman of colour,
the first black Governor-General."

Have I no colour,
I who was born white?
I blush in shades of rose,
tan like earth under sunlight.
My eyes are blue like a sparkling sea,
my lips, the colour of my blood and heart –
the same as anyone else's.

Am I a woman of no colour?

~ *Nellie P. Strowbridge*

If a baby is sick, pin the medal honouring the Virgin's Mother (St. Anne)
on the baby's clothing.

Accidental Newfie

The e-mail was brief and to the point. "Decision made – Permanent Residency status granted."

All the waiting and fretting is over. I'm bound for from England to Newfoundland to start my new life. What I'm letting myself in for will soon become a reality. I expected things would be different, and was ready to face new challenges, but what I found strangest were the small, almost insignificant differences that anyone from here would take for granted, but for me would at times, make me realise I was now a million miles - or so it felt like - from a life I'd grown accustomed to and simple tasks I used to complete automatically now required a degree of thought.

Consider some of the things you do without thinking. Driving. I had to remember to get into the "wrong" side of the car, drive on the "wrong" side of the road, avoid potholes and deal with other motorists who, for reasons best known to themselves, seem to think that the use of signal lights is an option.

Even the simple task of going into a shop and buying something required a degree of thought. First of all, the price on the item may not necessarily be the price you pay. (I was used to items being priced with the tax included.) Then I would reach into my pocket and reach for notes and coins that were unfamiliar in size and colour to me.

Even watching television had its challenges. I would see a football match (Yes, the game is called football not soccer, we invented it way before the game you call football was even thought of,) advertised to start at 7PM, sit down to watch the match and realise the advertised time was for a different time zone. This was another challenge I had to contend with – living in a country with different time zones.

I remember the day we moved into our new house. It was winter, very cold and snowing. My wife went to work, leaving me at home. I busied myself with various tasks, and as the morning went on the house was getting colder so I turned up the thermostat. This didn't seem to have much effect, but I put it down to not being used to the climate. At lunchtime my wife came home and noticed the house was a little chilly. I told her I'd cranked up the thermostat but maybe it was "teething" problems with a new house.

"Have you been putting wood in the furnace?" my wife enquired. Ah! Problem solved. Just another example of another challenge I would encounter. Heating was provided via a gas pipe that came though the wall. Turn it on and forget about it.

It's been a journey I've really enjoyed. One filled with stress, bewilderment, but mostly humour. A journey I would recommend to anyone – but why would you take it? You're already here.

By: Selwyn Skiiggs

Dieter's Paradox

It's strange, but we lose
whenever we win
In our on-going battle
to try and stay thin;

And, yet stranger still,
if we so choose,
We can say that we win
whenever we lose!

~ *David Elliott*
(1946- 2001)

After the ecumenical conference, three clergymen decided to go fishing in the pond near the lodge.

The Catholic priest said, "We're out of bait. I'll go to the lodge to get a refill." To the astonishment of the Pentecostal pastor, the priest stepped out of the boat and walked on top of the water all the way to the lodge.

The pastor thought, "What faith he must have! He can walk on the water! My faith is just as strong." He stepped out of the boat and fell in. The United Church minister hauled him back into the boat when he popped up for the third time.

A little later, the United Church minister said, "I could sure use a cold drink. I'll go up to the lodge to get us all one." He stepped out of the boat and walked on top of the water all the way to the lodge.

The pastor thought, "What faith he must have! He can walk on the water! My faith is must be stronger than his." He stepped out of the boat and fell in. The priest hauled him back into the boat when he popped up for the third time.

The minister passed around the bottles of water. The pastor said, "I have some chips to go with this." He took a deep breath, telling himself, "I can walk on the water. I can walk on the water." He was about to step over the side of the boat for the third time. The minister and the priest shrugged and pulled him back.

The priest said, "Don't get yourself all wet again. The rocks are on this side of the boat."

Connivers

Give an inch,
They take a mile,
And all the time,
They look at you
With a sneaky smile.

You can't point fingers
In their direction.
They always have an answer.
Their whole face brightens
With a smile that lingers.

Connivers, that's what they are.
In a subtle way,
They pull the wool
Over your eyes.
To them it's more play.

You can't get mad;
Twisted they may be.
It's a chance you take
When connivers are set free.
It's a game of wait and see.

It may be a long wait,
But that's the way it goes.
You have to make sure
You're a step ahead,
And nimble on your toes.

Connivers,
They'll get you
In the end,
With their scheming,
Then their screaming,
You're through.

~ Norma Jean House

Crime Pays

You woke me naked in my bed
With lumpy flesh and messed up head.
I tumbled to the cold, damp floor,
Stubbed my toe and loudly swore.

Yesterday's clothes were on the chair;
I had nothing else to wear
But this dirty shirt with a toothpaste stain.
What did I care? I'm not real vain.

I quickly left the wretched hole,
Along with all the stuff we stole.
You tossed it in your rusty heap.
We bumped away in that worn-out jeep.

Squirrels and bunnies were in our path.
I wanted to tell them all to scat.

I'm now in jail with clean clothes to wear.
Sometimes I manage to wash my hair.
I never want to leave this place.
All I do is stuff my face.

~ *Jean Legge Hiscock*

"She's a real sleeveen."
    A sleeveen is not to be trusted. A sleeveen may lead you into trouble and weasel out of it herself.

Early Morning Shower

Rolling over, I turned off my alarm before it started to beep. I hated the sound of it at 4:15 AM. It wasn't a civilized time for any human being to be crawling out of bed. As a camp manager, this was one of the fringe benefits. With paper-thin walls, the early to bed process doesn't really work when there's foot-traffic pounding the hallways all night long. Usually, it's pretty good but last night the noise was worse than usual which made for a sleepless night.

Reluctantly, I swung my legs out over the bunk, forcing myself to get up. Like a zombie, I fumbled for my toiletries and headed for the shower stalls. One of the first camp rules I learned was not to bang any doors in the wee hours of the morning. Wake up the workers and you would surely be on the hate list. The same workers didn't seem to care too much about making noise in the nighttime when the staff was trying to get some shut eye. To them that was irrelevant, regardless of the fact that we got up earlier than they did.

I quietly opened my room door, putting my slipper in between, so it wouldn't click or bang, creating noise – another camp quirk. My bedroom door was ajar; it didn't really matter, I had no treasures stashed in there. Anyway, the whole dorm was sleeping.

As I tiptoed down the hallway to the shower it was hauntingly eerie. The floor crunched at every door join and the tin roof cracked as the fans kicked in, blowing hot air towards the ceilings. One more left turn and I reached the ladies' shower room. All six stalls were empty. As I gazed into the mirror above the row of sinks in front of the showers, I wondered if I was playing with a full deck, committing myself to yet another camp job with three-score-plus years under my belt. Camp life is addictive. Once you try it, you're hooked, tending to go back whenever the opportunity arises. Being a camp staff worker, you work, eat and sleep in the same place, not having to go outside for anything only to come and go from camp on your days off. The hustle and bustle of the real world is left behind. Seclusion is part of the deal until your work term is completed. Camp accommodations, for the most part, is similar to living in a hotel room, everything provided except for your own personal items.

With no time for pondering, I crossed the floor, opened the shower stall door and went in. After hanging my towel on the hook, and placing my bathroom bag next to the garbage can, I turned the shower on to make sure it was warm by the time I was ready. I closed the stall door, stepped into the shower and pulled the curtain across.

As soon as the water hit my back my whole perspective changed. The water temperature was perfect, activating my brain, spelling out my agenda for me to tackle. Suddenly, I was revitalized, anxious to start a productive day. After turning the shower off, I placed a mat on the floor to stand on and reached for my towel to dry off, kind of hustling now before anybody got up. I always preferred to be done before all hands came to life. With so many people in camp aloneness is sacred, a rarity to be cherished. When dried, I wiped the shower down, opened the curtain and got out. Trying to dress in such a small area was a nuisance with nowhere to put anything. Now dressed and ready to start my day, with my gear in tow I reached out to open the shower stall door. Lo and behold, it wouldn't open.

For a minute it didn't register. I tried the knob again, to no avail. Stepping back, I sized it up and tried it again. Why wasn't it opening? Jiggling the knob in every direction, I began to panic. Being claustrophobic, my 4X4 space was starting to close in on me. My heart rate soared. Frantically, I dumped out my bathroom bag. I could find nothing to poke in the door to try and push back the latch to open it. Even the garbage can was empty. My thoughts of trying to push it open with my body were dashed when I realized the door swung in instead of out. Weren't all public doors supposed to swing out for safety reasons? The wall extending to the ceiling was completely boxed in. There was no escape window. By this time my hands were sweaty and I had to calm myself down by taking deep breaths and breathe properly.

I was totally confined!

The tantalizing roar of the vent fan created a white noise in the dead silence of the sleeping camp. I could not turn off the switch on the outside wall.

Nobody knew I was locked in the shower. My thoughts sent my brain into panic mode. Would I have a seizure from the pressure in my head, maybe a heart attack? My heart pounded like the beat of a drum. Nobody would be getting up for another hour. My sense of doom was growing. Not much good to start screaming for help since three walls separated me from the nearest bedroom. My closest acquaintance was the laundry room. The chance of anyone being there at 5 AM was slim. Doing laundry that early in the morning wasn't allowed because of people sleeping.

Like a jellyfish, I rummaged through my stuff on the floor. By this time, I was nauseated and I couldn't think straight under the constant roar of the fan. Q tips, shampoo, face cloth, toothbrush and a few more items lay under the towel on the floor. I grabbed my toothbrush and tried to push the handle in. It wouldn't fit. A glimmer of hope faded.

Would the camp attendant find me keeled over unconscious on the floor while she was doing her morning chores? Hysterically, I grabbed my bag and started shaking, hoping for a miracle. My lint brush fell out with my hair pick stuck to it. Could this be my lifeline?

I would have to try it. The pick was made of hard plastic with long, stiff teeth which would probably fit. Pushing several times, I jammed the pick in between the knob and the door box. As if I were deranged, with trembling sweaty hands, I began pushing and rooting with my pick in one hand and pulling with my other hand over and over, until I freed the lock. The door popped open. It seemed an eternity had passed!

My first full breath of air on the outside of the shower stall was as welcome as that of a newborn child, screaming for the first time. Now released, I could barely hold myself up to the sink counter to gain my composure. Trembling like a leaf, I somehow managed to dry my hair and brush my teeth before heading back to my room.

The hallways were still vacant. I reached my room, kicking my slipper aside, not worrying about who or how many people I woke when my bedroom door slammed. It took every fiber of my being to go out to the dining room for breakfast.

After a few cups of coffee, I settled down at our regular daily tool box meeting where tears flowed freely. After relating my story, I heard that a few other workers had also been locked in the stall and had managed to wiggle the door open. My solitary confinement was probably about the same duration as theirs. For me it had seemed endless.

Around camp, it was common knowledge that a lot of our doorknobs didn't work. I was positioned at the bottom of the totem pole. I was a new hire and a trainee camp manager and nobody had found it necessary to clue me in on this tidbit of useful information.

How ironic is it that something as petty as doorknobs would be defective in this multi-million-dollar project? What if the camp had a real emergency and several doors would not open? That would be a recipe for disaster. Sometimes the little things are overlooked for the finer things in life such as big screen televisions or all the goodies that's in the kitchen for lunch, the camp motto being: "Keep all clients happy."

The doorknob issue was on the maintenance list to be addressed right after the legs got repaired on the pool table in the entertainment room.

~ *Daisy Bennett-Lush*

"Buy a broom in May, brush your family away."
Wait until June to buy your broom to avoid death in your family

The Half Brother

I had a half brother once. He's dead now and buried in two different graves.

He was so big he had to be born in two pieces. The doctors couldn't figure out how to put him together and the lower half died soon anyway, so they buried it. The top half still lived so my father strapped a couple of two-by-fours about a foot long to his waist and he walked when he was only a day old.

As the two-by-fours wore down, or rather up, my father strapped longer pieces on him so by the time he was sixteen he was wearing eight-foot two-by-fours and had legs about six feet long. He managed very well with them and in high school even won the 100-yard dash by 90 yards.

One day he went out fishing and a beaver gnawed off one of his legs. He tumbled into the water and drowned. They buried the top half in a new grave rather than digging up his bottom half so he could be buried all together.

~ *Fred Stewart*
(1934 - 2007)

"Who knit ya?"
Who are your parents and what are your family connections?

The Glass of Pepsi

It feels cold and wet. When you shake the glass, the ice cubes make jingle-jangle music. The strong taste tickles my tongue and quenches my thirst.

I look around me as I take a sip. I see a closed Math book staring back, waiting to be opened.

I hear the sound of music blaring loudly from the stereo.

I take another sip of the glass of Pepsi.

~ *Stacey Hiscock-Pittman*

Written at a student workshop many years ago.

I heard that elephants paint their toenails red so they can hide away in cherry trees. Oh, you find that ridiculous, do you. Well, I bet you have never seen and elephant in a cherry tree, have you? See how well that disguise works!

Ed Dethroned!

A card shark he was proclaimed,
120's his game.
He couldn't be beaten and players retreated
Whenever he sat in for a game.

Still, they continued to come, big and small,
One by one, they all took the fall
As he constantly won game after game.

Then friends made in 2003,
Played with him enough you see
To catch onto his wiles with the cards.

Though, he continued to play a good hand,
And won on occasion, now and again,
It was with regret that he had to admit
when done,
It was only through sleight of hand,
he had usually won!

~ Marilyn Young

If you steal a slip from a flower, it will take root better than if it is given to you.

When the Deal Is Down

An elderly woman, wearing a money belt, was poised precariously on a narrow window ledge. She was deeply engrossed in conversation with a group of children as she shuffled a deck of cards.

The woman was arrested and charged with enticing passersby to gamble.

As she stood in the prisoners' dock the judge inquired if a lawyer had been assigned to represent her, to which the prisoner replied:

"Your Honour I don't believe I'm guilty, I have chosen to represent myself, I wish to take the stand and tell my story.

"I have travelled a long, lonely road. This deck of cards has been a faithful companion, sir, and the calendar has been my sanity journal."

THE ACE:

"You see your Honour as I gaze at the Ace, memories flood my mind of times I walked through rain, wind, and blinding snow to reach our little one-room school where one teacher taught every grade and every subject. I was a hard worker and dreamt of someday becoming a politician who would bring a little good news to the people of my island home."

THE TWO:

"As I view the deuce, I recall a period of confusion. I was a whiz in science. One day I was two hours late for an appointment. Following my inquiry, sir, I learned our clocks had been set ahead two hours in an attempt to save daylight time in 1988. Somewhere, sir, someone missed a quantum leap."

THE THREE:

"As I look at the three I see visions of ballot boxes everywhere in Newfoundland. In some places they have big celebrations; in other places they are grinding their teeth. I then recall, sir, it was the third month, 1949. After that, my sisters and brothers were given a new identity. Our independent country became one of the ten provinces of the Dominion of Canada."

THE FOUR:

"As I hold the four, your Honour, I see in a wooded area of Newfoundland, the winter of 1822-23, three scantily dressed, freezing, starving Beothuk women begging, with bared breasts, for food on Easter Saturday. The youngest screamed wildly as she saw her long-lost father attempting to cross a frozen pond to join the family. Pursued by hunters the father fell through the ice and drowned."

THE FIVE:

"Holding the five, sir, I see images of five Newfoundland men retired from the political battlefield. Above each image, I see the names of Joey, Frank, Tom, Brian, and Clyde."

THE SIX:

"Your Honour, I tremble as I gaze at the six. I stayed abreast of world affairs. I still sense an overwhelming power of joy and anticipation as I recall six men and, the first ever citizen observer, a woman, boarding a space shuttle. Within minutes the world was plunged into a deep state of shock when the *Challenger* exploded."

THE SEVEN:

"As I hold the seven, beautiful memories of childhood games flood my memory bank. However, the weight of my money belt forces me back to reality. It was the seventh month, 1987, your honour, when our national leader, using a Robert Carmichael's motif, endorsed a loonie idea. It was indeed, sir, a heavy loonie idea valued at about seventy-two cents American."

THE EIGHT:

"Today, sir, I can relive the joy in my community on the fourteenth of the eight month, nineteen hundred and forty-one, when a great document, containing eight common principles based on hopes for a better future for the world, was signed by two world leaders aboard the U.S.S Augusta off Newfoundland. Twenty-six states of the United Nations later endorsed the principles in Washington, D.C."

THE NINE:

"I shudder as I hold the nine. My sisters and brothers of my island home live in morbid fear of poverty because of government deficits. Yet looking back it was the ninth month, nineteen hundred eighty-seven, when our national leader hosted a meeting with forty-one leaders of French-speaking nations and Territories, forgiving three hundred and twenty-five million dollars in loans to the poorest participants. Your honour, since we ae indexed as the poorest, I live in hope our national leaders still believe in forgiveness now, as they did then."

THE TEN:

"Memories darken as I gaze at the ten. I honour the men and women who fought that we might live in peace. Many did not return to their island home, and those who did probably hold emotions that no one, other than their comrades, could scarcely understand. Yet every Newfoundlander understood the pain of the families of victims who met with tragedy on the fourteenth day, of the tenth month, nineteen forty-two. Living in peace, your honour, has extracted a high price. The *Caribou* with its 137 passengers was sunk by a German U-boat."

THE JACK:

"My wrinkles turn into deep lines of laughter, sir, as I hold the Jack. As children we were not allowed to play gambling games. One childhood game till tickles my fancy. Three Jacks were removed from a deck of cards. Then each player was dealt an equal number of cards. Drawing from each other's hand, clockwise, we had to throw

214

out our pairs. The one who drew the Jack was classed as the Jack-Ass. Thus, being classed as the Jack-Ass. It was great fun being a Jack-Ass in my day, sir. That seems to have changed today, Your Honour. Or, then again, has it?"

THE QUEEN:

"When John Cabot, first came to Newfoundland, sir, our waters were teeming with fish. In my younger days, a woman from my native home, Marie Penney, was deeply involved in the fishery. Our nation recognized her great contribution to society, Your Honour, and she was bestowed the title "Queen of the Fisheries." That, sir, was indeed a true sign of gender equity."

THE KING:

"Our island, sir, is a history book not yet fully tapped. There are many forms of kings and not necessarily of royal descent. One such man gave life and hope to millions of people the world over and it was an outport area in Newfoundland, nineteen forty-one where this king shed his life's blood on our shoes. The world will forever pay homage to Sir Fredrick Banting, the co-discoverer of insulin. His plane crashed near Musgrave Harbour and he died a day later."

FOUR SUITS:

"You will note, sir, as I shuffle the deck of cards it has four suits. In my younger days, crones earned a few pennies foretelling people's future. Diamonds, Your Honour, represented wealth and riches; hearts foretold love and happiness; spades spoke of sorrow; clubs indicated one's future labours; I sometimes feel the crones erred in reading my future."

COLOURS:

"The deck contains only two colours, sir, red and black. I hold great respect for both colours. Whenever the red blood stopped flowing through the veins of a loved one, we showed respect by donning the black for a full year. Black was a colour I donned early in life, sir."

40 "WITHOUT" PICTURES:

"I show you forty cards from the deck "without" pictures. Faith was so strong in my island home that we fasted for the forty days of Lent to commemorate a great man who spared Newfoundlanders, and others, from the tortures of Hell."

12 "WITH" PICTURES

"Here, Your Honour, are twelve cards "with" pictures. We highly honoured the one who saved us from the fires of Hell; so much so that we celebrated His birthday with twelve days of bellsnickling, dancing, and visiting every home in our community. Can you, sir, imagine the strengths of Newfoundland families and communities to spend twelve days together in on-going festivities?"

FIFTY-TWO CARDS:

"I hold before you, sir, a deck of cards comprised of fifty-two in total. Almost all businesses now use the Julian calendar. I show you this "fixed calendar."

'I often ponder why this universe, so steeped in financial crisis, considers the fixed calendar too radical to accept. You see, Your Honour, the fixed calendar consists of thirteen months. Each month has twenty-eight days, making it four weeks in each month. A total of fifty-two weeks in a year.

'The newest act for unemployment insurance is four hundred and twenty hours of employment. If one half of our communities were employed sixteen hours a day, for twenty-six and one quarter days, that half would qualify for a paid rest, while the other half would pick up and work their twenty-six and one quarter days, sixteen hours per day. That sir, would be job-sharing and equality. It behooves me how to persuade religious and civil groups, astronomers and navigators how to end their opposition to the fixed calendar. Such a simple solution to such a great problem."

JOKER:

"We have one final card in each deck, sir. As you can see, by using the fixed calendar you would find that every four years we would have one extra day without a name. The fixed calendar, similar

216

to the Julian, has the same names from Sunday to Saturday. I therefore feel that if my dreams of being a politician had matured I would seek to call a world-wide holiday on that spare day, and I would choose to name it Joker's Day.

'Webster's Thesaurus states that a joker is also known as a Jester, a comic and a fool. It was my intention that a woman of my age could play because the joker rules during the 500th anniversary of John Cabot. As I sat on the window ledge, prior to being arrested, I was merely testing passersby on their knowledge of our island's history by using a deck of cards. Am I guilty of enticing the public to gamble? I trust, sir, you know of our history. I therefore leave the decision of my fate in your hands. I, therefore, rest my case in your honour. The deal is done."

Thank you.

Written in 1997 for the 500th anniversary celebration of John Cabot's expedition to North America.

~ *Minnie J. Vallis*
(1933 - 2013)

You know a person's shoes are not paid for when they squeak.

Through the Eyes of an Angel

When I was younger, everyone always told me I was too critical. Susan Rodgers, critical?

"I don't think so," was my reply. Maybe I do tend to find fault with an occasional person. Okay. Okay. I am a little critical. Isn't everyone critical at times? My best friend thought I should try to look at things from a different perspective, through the eyes of someone else for a day. I wasn't thrilled at the idea, but it would be a great topic for my next article. I work as a reporter for the local newspaper in the suburbs of New York.

Well, here I am now, sitting in this park, trying to document my thoughts and get some insight into the lives of others. My friend, Mark, thinks this will do me a world of good. I can't see myself being transformed into a new person overnight. I lift my head from my writing and look around for someone to scrutinize.

I notice an older man walking down the path carrying a paper bag, probably a bottle of rum. He may be a homeless bum. He is dressed in a woolen sweater and women's jeans and shoes. I guess they came from a charity organization. He stops and asks two teenage boys for money. They laugh and walk away. Who will condemn them for not wanting to support his alcoholic habits?

I put down my pen and watch him make his way through the alley and disappear around a corner. I want to find out more about this old man. You know what they say: curiosity killed the cat. Maybe, I'll go and talk with him; it won't hurt to see what he has to say. I quickly stand up and smooth down my baby blue blazer and black skirt. I should have dressed more casually for this research assignment, but you never know who you may run into on the street.

I move quickly around the corner into the alley, realizing that I've never been through this part of town on foot. The area is fairly unfamiliar to me. I reach into my pocket and pull out a mini tape recorder hoping the old man will let me interview him for my article.

As I walk through the alley, I notice lots of other people, dressed shabbily. My eyes dart quickly around looking for him. My gaze falls upon a little child with matted hair and dirty skin. He is wearing a faded Ninja turtle t-shirt and shorts. The poor boy must be freezing. I stop and watch him. A tear trickles down my cheek as I watch him dig through a garbage can. He smiles as he picks up a half-eaten piece of pizza. He gnaws it hungrily. I can't imagine a little child having to live this way. When he turns around to look me, his smile tugs at my heart strings.

Then, I catch a glimpse of the old man I was looking for. He is sitting on the ground smoking a cigarette. I walk over to him cautiously, not wanting to startle him.

Softly, I ask, "Will you speak with me for a few minutes?"

I see a flash of terror in his eyes. He asks, "Are you a police officer?"

"No. You can relax. I'm a journalist who would like to ask you a few questions for an article."

We sat on a battered wooden staircase. I asked him about his life and jotted down notes as we talked.

Soon, his sweet, funny charm was making me smile. He told me that his name was Maurice and he was sixty-seven. The streets had been his home for over 20 years.

"I'm doing fine now in the summer," he said.

He pointed to a cardboard box nestled under the steps. "See, I even have a roof over my head. Until it rains."

"How did you end up living this way?" I asked.

"It was one thing after another. I lost my job. My house burnt down the same month and my home insurance company went bankrupt. I lost everything. It's not easy finding your way up after the hole gets so deep. After a while, it even gets comfortable. I never planned to live on the streets, you know. It's not exactly a childhood dream."

We sat together until the sun sank low in the sky and the alley grew dark. He told me about his happy days as a boy, about his years as a young man.

I became intrigued by his stories. I'd dismissed him as a nobody, without knowing anything about his life. I felt a stab of guilt.

When I stood up and expressed my gratitude to him for his time, he held my hand tightly.

"Thank you for listening, Miss. Come back, anytime."

219

"I promise I will come to see you again, Maurice," I said. "Wait here. I'll get you a coffee from the café around the corner."

I paid for the two coffees and bagels and rushed back to the alley. I felt different; I felt good about myself.

In the alley, I looked around for Maurice. The old man was nowhere to be found. I checked his cardboard box. It was empty. I saw a note addressed to "Miss Journalist" taped on its side. My hands shook as I quickly opened up the letter: I read:

Deal as gently with the faults of others as you do with your own. Maurice

I stared blankly at the letter. My eyes filled with tears. Maurice was a sweet old man. I had only talked to one street person and I already felt that the course of my life had changed. I needed to find Maurice to tell him I did care, to thank him for helping me to understand people better. I had no idea where he'd gone.

I described him to an older woman in the alley. I gave her his name.

"I don't know anyone called Maurice," she said. "He's not anyone who hangs around here." She shrugged and crawled into Maurice's box.

I asked everyone I saw about Maurice. I found nothing, but blank faces and puzzled looks. It seemed as though he didn't even exist.

I slowly walked back to the café, keeping my eye out for Maurice. I sat at an outside table and sipped a cafe mocha. I stared blankly at my journal. What would I write? Who was that old man? Where did he come from? My mind whirled with confusion. I couldn't piece anything together.

Whoever he was, I wanted to thank him for opening my eyes to a side of life I had never considered. I remembered the little boy I had seen earlier in the alley. I decided to go back to look for him. I finished my café mocha.

In the alley, I noticed the little boy sitting by himself in a dark corner. I went over and spoke softly to him, the way adults often speak to a young child: "Where do you live?"

"Out here. I have friends, you see. We tell each when we find a good place to sleep and where the best dumpsters are. It's not so bad."

"Where are your parents?"

"We used to live over there." He pointed to a rundown building, most of the windows broken. "One day I came home from school and Mom and Dad were gone. I heard they are dead. Maybe they just had to get away from the man who came around asking them for his money." He shrugged. "I'm on my own. I know that for sure. I don't go inside."

My chest tightened as if my heart was going to explode. I tried to conceal my tears. I held out my hand. "Do you want to come home with me?"

"Do you have a roof that don't leak? It's going to rain tonight."

"I do. What's your name?"

"Jacob." He put his small hand in mine and we walked away from the alley together. It's hard to explain. I'd known this little boy for such a short time. He filled a spot in my heart I had not known was empty. As a single woman, I'd have to work hard to convince authorities to let me keep him. I knew I would figure out a way to care for him. I had room in my apartment and in my heart for this little boy

As we walked by the café, I noticed a sign on the door. The heading said: *Thought for the Day*. I stopped to read it.

"Be kind to strangers. For some who have done this have entertained angels without realizing it."

I repeated that quote over and over in my mind. I looked down at Jacob with his dark hair and bright eyes. His features resembled mine a little. I smiled. I felt warm, filled by a ray of sunshine.

I sit here now 12 years after the day when I was visited by my guardian angel, Maurice. After the day we met, I opened up to others and did whatever I could to help anyone in need. I never again judged a book by its cover or a person by the clothing he wore.

Today, I watch my son, Jacob, climb the stairs to the podium to accept his high school diploma. The salty taste of tears hits my lips and I whisper softly, "Thank you, Maurice." I believe he hears me. Without my guardian angel, I would never have found Jacob, my other angel.

~ *Terry-Lynn Shugarue*

God Speaks

Under my clouds,
Above my sea,
My creation lives.
My people know me.

Farther from Hell,
Closer to land,
My creation longs
To hold my hand.

After I know,
Before you do
Creation hear me.
I'm coming to you.

~ *Natasha Strickland*

Faith

Faith is the key to Heaven
Oh, Father, grant once more to men
A simple childlike faith again,
Forgetting colour, race and creed,
Seeing only the heart's deep need.
For faith alone can save man's soul
And lead him to a higher goal,
For there's but one unfailing course
We win by faith and not by force.

~ *G. M Legge*

Fellowship

I have schizophrenia. Saying that is not easy. But when Page One decides to publish a book, they call on me. I have no words to convey how that makes me feel about myself. To be included in putting a book together. I have no words, just an overwhelming sense of gratitude to be included, to be a part of something bigger then me: the kindness of others goes a long way in making me feel good about myself. Sometimes a little goes a long way.

Having my writing published makes me realize I am not alone. I have friends who care, who place a value on what I write. From the bottom of my heart I thank you for helping me; nobody else can do what you do. Thank you for including me; you know what it means to me I will always be here to help. It is by helping other people we find ourselves in the process. I've made a lot of mistakes in my life things I can't explain, things I'd rather forget.

The one thing that makes me feel normal is writing. I'm shy and mostly reclusive, but when I write I feel good. Lots of people draw the wrong conclusions. That's something I have no interest in anymore. The thing is: if people knew the real me, they would conclude, this guy is a survivor. If they knew me the way Page One members know me, if they would include me, they would find out that beneath it all is a guy who is real, an idealist trying to set a good example. Trying to forget the past and look forward to the future.

Having lived my entire life in Deer Lake, it is not easy, but that's life. I love my home I would rather be here than anywhere else.

Someday, I pray people will see the real me. Not the schizophrenic me. The good Lord justified me and set me free; that is His gift to me. Open up and you may receive his gifts, too.

~ *Dana Cole*

Imagine

They say that there's no limit to human imagination,
That all the possibilities and impossibilities of the universe
Exist in our heads, if only we could grab them,
With fingers fragile like crystal glass, but networked like forest
roots,
We imagined going to the moon and we made it so,
We pictured the bottom of the sea and delved into inky black
depths,
We imagine the monsters that plague our dreams and hide what
real monstrosity is,
We visualize, we randomize, we create and sculpt the clay of our
minds,
And despite all this, I ask of you,
Can you invent for me a new colour?
Of all the things in the universe, all the things we can apparently
create,
Did you ever stop and wonder why our scope is limited to seven?
Infrared and ultraviolet boxes in our colour spectrum,
Yet according to imagination that shouldn't matter,
So if there is no limit, and the reality is obsolete,
If I try hard enough then those seven should by rights become
eight.
I focus deeply digging through my mind, no dusty corner left
behind,
And upon my mental horizon I see something new,
Something incredible, something way beyond blue....

~ Brittney Stuckless

225

The Special Light

I lie there dead, or so it seems.
The tunnel ahead is the colour of dreams.
In the distance, not far away
I see the floor where skeletons lie.
I pass the bodies, pass the screams.
I see a light that silently gleams.
Gaining courage, I overcome fright,
Make my way toward the light.

As I walk further, my eyes grow wider.
My body's the horse, my mind the rider.
When I get closer, I push with all my might;
The sun is blinding; I close my eyes tight.
The force is greater than anything I could think.
I'm pulled straight forward and then I begin to sink

Shouldn't I go up to Heaven with God?
I see the heavenly spirit; she gives me a nod.
I guess it's all over; the trip was so long.
I'm back on Earth, where I belong.

~ *Julie Crocker*

Cemetery Road

Would you want to live your life on Cemetery Road
And watch the bier bear lifeless load
Of president or pauper
On his final trip to his last abode,

And contemplate man's mindless race
At ever greater speed to grave embrace,
The treadmill ever faster
And at the end to leave no trace?

The rich man's name in stone is hewn,
It's but a necropolis-tic rune,
And only for a little while
Time erodes the words of doom.

Billions born, their fate entwined,
Forgotten, gone, life unsigned.
Certain that through time,
Rich man, poor man, lost to mind.

Lives that led with pompous blow
In Palace Hall or on Skid Row,
In the grave are all akin,
At the end of Cemetery Road.

September 25, 2017

~ John Tuach

Guest of Honour

I am the guest of honour,
The center of attention,
My hair expertly styled,
Make-up meticulously applied.

So many have come,
Not just Harry Flint
Who goes to every Wake
To get away from the scorching July heat.
Everyone knows
Funeral homes have the best air-conditioning.

They all greet each other,
But it's me they want to see,
Me so smartly dressed,
Some say I look as if I'm sleeping.

How silly!
I sleep with my mouth wide open,
And snore loudly.

How carefully I planned everything:
The flowers, the service.
I planned it all, even paid for it.

Later though, I needed money
For important things: cigarettes and slot machines.
I borrowed against my funeral
meaning to pay it back.

The cheapskates!
They took me out of my fancy casket
And put me in this.
I'm so ashamed.
I want to get up and join my friends,

Telling stories, running their fingers through my hair,
Messing it up, laughing.

And they kiss me.
I lie still and let them
'Cause I am the guest of honour.

~ Jean Legge Hiscock

If you hear of one death, you will soon hear of two more. A fourth funeral foretells six wakes.

Roxanne Abbott
Florence Antle
Cynthia Babb Fry
Arthur Ball*
Daisy Bennett-Lush
Karen Bennett
Ray Bennett
Anne Bowring
Sarah-Lynn Bussey
Dana Cole
Kayla Critch
Julie Crocker
Candice Curlew
Shirley Dyke
David Elliott*
P. J. Fernandez
Annie Gilliard*
Terry Gordon
Vaughn Harbin
Terri Hayden (Moores)
Deborah Hedd (a.k.a. D. Jean Young)
Stacey Hiscock-Pittman
Norma Jean House
Myrtle Hutchings
Edith Johnson*
Aaron Kawaja
Victoria Young. Kawaja
Francis King
Hilda King*
Trina King
Julia LeClair
G. M. Legge
Jean Legge Hiscock
Mike Madigan
Terry Manuel*
Deanna Mcdeiros
Angela Parsons
Robert Parsons

Samantha A. Parsons
Marjorie Patey
Delaney Pelley
Blanche Penney (a.k.a. Nico LaBlanc)*
Daphne Russell
Desmond Russell
Jackie Sheppard Alcock
Terri-Lynn Shugarue
Selwyn Skiggs
Ronald T. Smith*
Matthew Spence
Fred Stewart*
Natasha Strickland
Nellie P. Strowbridge
Brittney Stuckless
Jamie Stuckless
Jennifer Sutton
John Tuach
George T. Tucker
Minnie J. Vallis*
Marilyn Young
Ruth Young*

*These contributors are now contributing creativity to the world beyond this one.